Just Looking

JOHN UPDIKE

Just Looking

ESSAYS ON ART

with a new foreword by the author

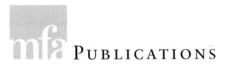

PUBLICATIONS

a division of the

Museum of Fine Arts, Boston

for Judith Jones
whose nice idea this was

and with gratitude to my art teachers
Clinton Shilling   Carlton Boyer
Hyman Bloom   Percy Horton

seeing is believing

This edition first published in 2001 by
MFA PUBLICATIONS
a division of the Museum of Fine Arts, Boston
295 Huntington Avenue
Boston, Massachusetts 02115

Published by arrangement with Alfred A. Knopf, a division of Random House, Inc.

Some of the essays included in this work were originally published in *The New Republic,*
The New York Times Book Review, Réalités, Travel & Leisure, Vanity Fair, and *ZEITmagazin.*
Art & Antiques: "What MOMA Done Tole Me," "American Children," "Yankee Seer"
("Field's Luminous Folk"), and "Some Rectangles of Blue." *The New Yorker*: "A Case of Melancholia."
Grateful acknowledgment is made to Harry N. Abrams, Inc., for permission to reprint John Updike's
foreword from *Doubly Gifted: The Author as Visual Artist* by Kathleen G. Hjerter.
Copyright © 1986 by Harry N. Abrams, Inc. Reprinted by permission.

ISBN 0-87846-577-4
Library of Congress Card Number: 00-107965

Available through D.A.P. / Distributed Art Publishers
155 Sixth Avenue, 2nd floor
New York, New York 10013
Tel.: 212 627 1999 · Fax: 212 627 9484

FIRST PAPERBACK EDITION
10 9 8 7 6 5 4 3 2

Printed and bound in Italy

Acknowledgments

"A City Frieze," "Little Lightnings," "The Apple's Fresh Weight," "Working Space," "Moving Along," "A Case of Overestimation," and "The Hand of Saint Saens" first appeared in the American edition of *Réalités*. "American Children" and "Some Rectangles of Blue" were written for that magazine shortly before it ceased publication in the spring of 1981, and they eventually came out in *Art and Antiques*. "Violence at the Windows," "Is Art Worth It?," "Something Missing," "Heavily Hyped Helga," and "Reluctant Butterfly" ran as reviews of art shows in *The New Republic*. "An Outdoor Vermeer" first appeared in *Travel and Leisure*; "A Mischievous Monet" in *Vanity Fair*; "Field's Luminous Folk" and "What MoMA Done Tole Me" in *Art and Antiques*; "A Case of Melancholia" in *The New Yorker*; and "A Case of Solicitude" in *ZEITmagazin*, translated into German, as No. 1 of the "Zeitmuseum der 100 Bilder." "The Child Within" reviewed *A Treasury of the Great Children's Book Illustrators,* by Susan E. Meyer, for *The New York Times Book Review,* and "Writers and Artists" served as an introduction to *Doubly Gifted: The Author as Visual Artist,* edited by Kathleen G. Hjerter. The *Réalités* essays, plus "An Outdoor Vermeer" and "Violence at the Windows," were published in a limited edition by Sylvester & Orphanos, of Los Angeles, in 1985, under the title *Impressions*. I thank Toula Polygalaktos, Kathy Zuckerman, and Edward Douglas for tracking down permissions on the reproductions in *Just Looking,* and Karl H. Klein for generously providing information about his uncle Ralph Barton.

Contents

Foreword to the MFA Edition

"Just Looking" was originally published by Alfred A. Knopf, Inc., in 1989. Although my childhood passion was graphic art — comic strips, comic books, magazine cartoons, movie animations — my exposure to high art, as the first essay here states, was slight. I became an art critic so casually, with so just a diffidence as to my competence, that the collection of these incidental pieces had to be prompted by the suggestion of someone else. Judith Jones, my long-time editor at Knopf, made the suggestion; her then assistant Kathy Zuckerman labored patiently at securing the many required permissions and transparencies; and Peter Andersen, the volume's designer, meticulously and inventively arranged each page. The publication of such a book is a far more elaborate and cooperative venture than that of a sheaf of poetry or prose; its re-publication, re-engaging the old problems of permission fees and faithful reproduction, is scarcely to be thought of. Imagine my surprise and pleasure, then, when I was informed that a publishing house newly created under the auspices of Boston's Museum of Fine Arts wished to reissue this, my lone art book, in the new century.

Manufactured in Italy, it enjoyed an optimistically large printing that generated, for a time, an excess of copies. But those copies gradually disappeared, and I have more than once had to resort to my own dwindling stock to supply the occasional seeker of this title. For me, *Just Looking* retains the value of a scrapbook, a souvenir of happy hours spent in contemplation of art, whether hanging in museums or, as with the shorter pieces commissioned by the short-lived American version of *Réalités*, clipped from magazines. Assembling so various a scrapbook had its challenges. Ralph Barton's lovely black-and-white wash illustrations for the 1928 Boni & Liveright edition of Balzac's *Droll Stories*, I remember, had to have their touch of magenta filled in by Peter Andersen's own hand, and my search for photographs of Jean Ipoustéguy's sculpture took me deep into the Fogg Museum's basement archives. These two essays, on Barton and Ipoustéguy, were my original, unsolicited ideas — my most arduous ventures into appraisal and research. Though Barton was a keen Francophile, and these illustrations constituted an act of homage, the Barton pages were eliminated from *Un simple regard: Essais sur l'art* (Horay, 1990), the only edition in a foreign language with which *Just Looking* was favored. *Le Monde*'s reviewer (under the heading "*Le regard froid du dilettante*") said testily, of the twenty pages I devoted to France's own Ipoustéguy, "*C'est trop.*"

A by no means unfriendly American notice in *The New York Times Book Review* by the esteemed art critic and philosopher Arthur C. Danto chastised me for including a few of my own youthful drawings and characterized many of the pieces as "ekphrasis" — that is, not criticism at all, yielding only "enhanced understanding of the writer, and his or her preoccupations." Danto also noted (again, in friendly fashion) that my essays would not "hold great urgency for those whose concerns with art connect with the great critical issues of today." What those issues, now the issues of yesterday, or the day before, were, he did not have space to spell out — but it is true that I penned my impressions from well outside the art establishment, the New York "scene," and the transatlantic art market. For me, regressively enough, something broadly called "beauty" must attach to art, along with an aspiration to permanence. The deliberately ugly and impermanent make me look away. Such an attitude may be outmodedly dandyish, given the industrial heat and machinations within the mills of the art business, including the art-crit business, but to Danto's gentle charge of being "an artistic *flâneur*" I can only plead the examples of Baudelaire and Henry James, who both published frequent observations about the visual arts near the outset of this long period in which these arts have led the way, have been the most spectacular and fresh of human expressions, have most brilliantly sought the tune for modernity to dance to.

Looking at pictures takes less time than reading a book or listening to music. It tells us something even at a glance. These pages preserve a succession of glances and, in their unsteady wake, reflections. It was to the MFA that, nearly fifty years ago, I travelled from across the Charles in company with a Radcliffe student, a Fine Arts major, and watched her circle and ponder, notebook in hand, a little, well-lit, headless Attic sphinx. Fitting it is, then, that this same museum should undertake to reissue my encounters with a parade of glowing sphinxes.

— J. U.

APRIL 2000

Just Looking

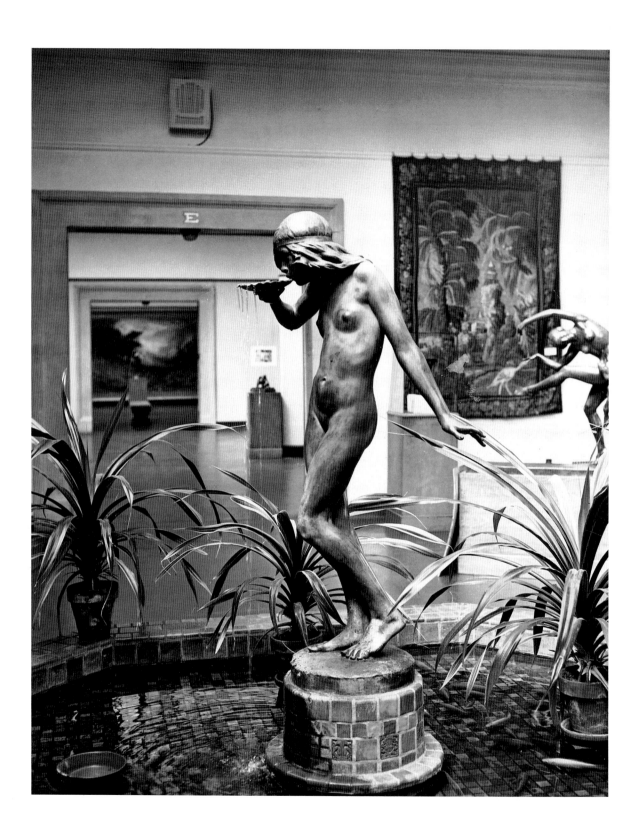

What MoMA Done Tole Me

Once I lived in New York City, for twenty brief months, though as a child I had dreamed of spending my adult life there. My father's sister lived in Greenwich, Connecticut, and on one of my visits to her house she took me into the city to the Museum of Modern Art, and later claimed that she had never seen a child so interested in the place. I was around twelve at the time. My experience of museums had been limited to the Reading Museum, which lay a pleasant summer walk of two miles from our town in Pennsylvania. I have described the museum in a short story, written in 1962, titled "Museums and Women," and under the convenient post-modern rubric of "appropriation" here quote myself at length:

> My first museum I would visit with my mother. It was a provincial museum, a stately pride to the third-class inland city it ornamented. It was approached through paradisaical grounds of raked gravel walks, humus-fed plantings of exotic flora, and trees wearing tags, as if freshly christened by Adam. The museum's contents were disturbingly various, its cases stocked with whatever scraps of foreign civilization had fallen to it from the imperious fortunes of the steel and textile barons of the province. A shredding kayak shared a room with a rack of Polynesian paddles. A mummy, its skull half masked in gold, lay in an antechamber like one more of the open-casket funerals common in my childhood. Miniature Mexican villages lit up when a switch was flicked, and a pyramid was being built by dogged brown dolls

Edward McCartan
The Drinking Girl, c. 1925
Bronze fountain, height 59½″
The Reading Public Museum and Art Gallery, Reading, Pennsylvania

who never pulled their papier-mâché stone a fraction of an inch. An infinitely patient Chinaman, as remote from me as the resident of a star, had carved a yellow rhinoceros horn into an upright crescental city, pagoda-tipped, of balconies, vines, and thimble-sized people wearing microscopic expressions of pain.

This was downstairs. Upstairs, up a double flight of marble climaxed by a green fountain splashing greenly, the works of art were displayed. Upstairs, every fall, the county amateur artists exhibited four hundred watercolors of peonies and stone barns. The rest of the year, somberly professional oils of rotting, tangled woodland had the walls to themselves, sharing the great cool rooms with cases of Philadelphia silver, chests decorated with hearts, tulips, and bleeding pelicans by Mennonite folk artists, thick aqua glassware left bubbled by the blowing process, quaint quilts, and strange small statues. Strange perhaps only in the impression they made on me. They were bronze statuettes, randomly burnished here and there as if by a caressing hand, of nudes or groups of nudes. The excuse for nudity varied; some of the figures were American Indians, some were mythical Greeks. One lady, wearing a refined, aloof expression, was having her clothes torn from her by a squat man with horns and hairy hooved legs hinged the wrong way. Another statue bodied forth two naked boys wrestling. Another was of an Indian, dressed in only a knife belt, sitting astride a horse bareback, his chin bowed to his chest in sorrow, his exquisitely toed feet hanging down both hard and limp, begging to be touched. I think it was the smallness of these figures that carried them so penetratingly into my mind. Each, if it could have been released into life, would have stood about twenty inches high and weighed in my arms perhaps as much as a cat. I itched to finger them, to interact with them, to insert myself into their mysterious silent world of strenuous contention—their bulged tendons burnished, their hushed violence detailed down to the fingernails. They were in their smallness like secret thoughts of mine projected into dimension and permanence, and they returned to me as a response that carried strangely into parts of my body. I felt myself a furtive animal stirring in the shadow of my mother.

This inventory excludes a larger statue on the second floor, who had already been given her sentences in a novel, *The Centaur,* from that same 1962: "In the center of the large oval room at the head of the stairs a naked green lady, life size, stood in the center of a circular black-lipped pool. She was a fountain. She held to her lips a scallop shell of bronze and her fine face was pursed to drink, but the mechanics of the fountain dictated that water should spill forever from the edge of the shell away from her lips. . . . As a child I was troubled by her imagined thirst, and I would

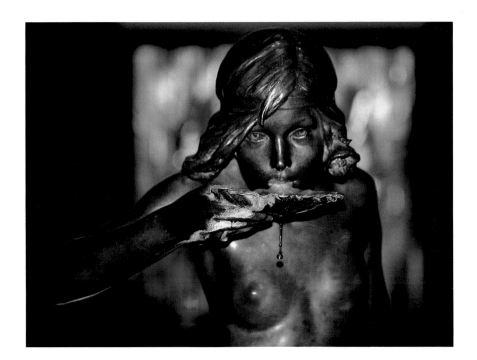

McCartan
The Drinking Girl (detail)

place myself so I could see the enduring inch that held her mouth from contact with the water. . . . The patience of her wait, the mildness of its denial, seemed unbearable to me then, and I told myself that when darkness came, and the mummy and the Polynesian masks and the glass-eyed eagles below were sealed in shadow, then her slim bronze hand made the very little motion needed, and she drank."

These marmoreal impressions of frozen figures sharing a hushed mansion with mummies, of art as a somewhat erotic mode of death, were formed in contrast to the lively commercial arts of the Thirties and Forties—the comic strips, the magazine illustrations, the animated cartoons, the hand-lettered signs, the kitschy wood carvings and slapdash stage backdrops turned out in his crowded studio by our spry neighbor across the street, Clint Shilling, the local artist, who gave me, at my mother's request, drawing and painting lessons. Something of this larger, cartoonish artistic atmosphere must have seemed captured in the Museum of Modern Art, for I did not feel oppressed within it—instead I felt landed upon a shore of that radiant island open to the sky, that uplifted paradise of penthouses, flashing lights, streamlined decors, and tilted top

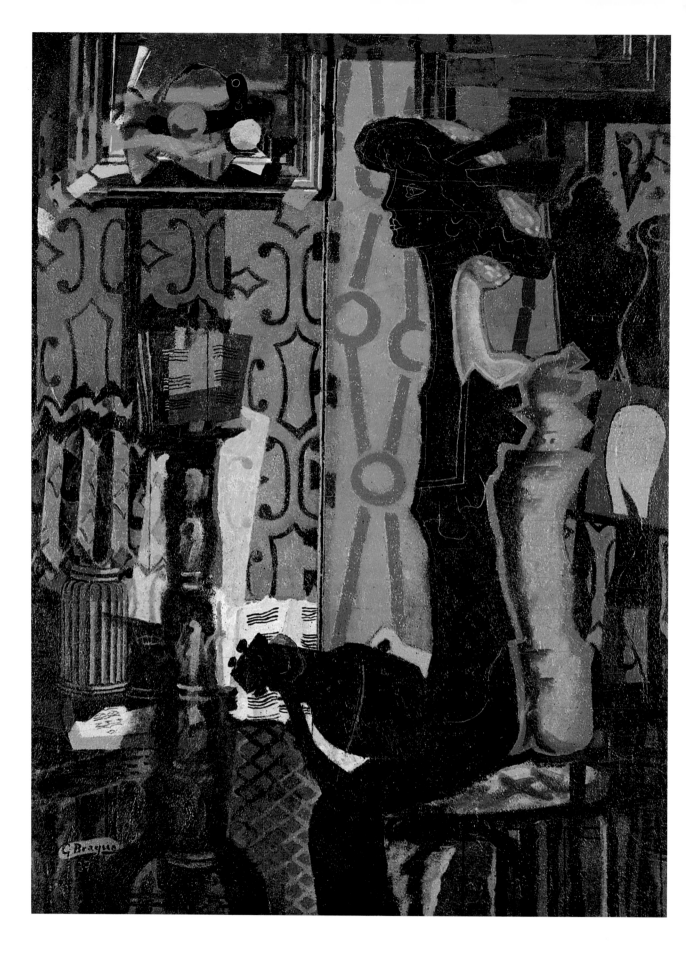

hats which was what Hollywood presented to the masses, usually with musical accompaniment, as New York City.

The contents of the museum would seem staid now. The work I most surely remember is Braque's *Woman with a Mandolin,* painted in 1937, in a Cubist style long liberated from its original brown tones and studiously fractured planes. A thin woman in insubstantial silhouette, as if cut out of black tin that was then hastily scratched with a few lines indicating an eye, lips, hair, an ear, and an earring, could barely be distinguished among a tall jumble of bright wallpapery snippets which included a painting of a painting and a music stand much too large for its music. I did not yet have my full growth, for the woman of black tin towered over me like the green lady forever trying to drink, and with some of the same frozen sadness. She seemed lost there, pinned, and I could not understand why the artist had rendered her so carelessly and immersed her in such chaotic surroundings; yet the work made upon me a paradoxical impression of dignity, of clear intention: we were not just dealing with bad drawing. The ornate wide frame, in those days long before the wise heads of MoMA opted for narrow frames of mock bamboo, reinforced the dignity, the impression that the lack, if a lack existed, was mine. And I was charmed (if I can reconstruct an aesthetic reaction over forty years old) by the painting's freedom and impudence; I was pleased that something like this could be done.

From that initiatory visit I seem to remember, too, a construction of paper and string high on the wall like a kite tucked into an attic, and the white bas-relief of Arp's called *Bell and Navels,* its blobby three-fingered shape perhaps reassuringly reminding me of Mickey Mouse's gloved hand, which also had but three fingers. I felt myself, in my aunt's shadow, moving through a kind of toy store, where the toys could not be bought or touched, only admired—toys not gloomily handed down from past ages, like Polynesian paddles and carved rhinoceros horns, but cheerfully hammered and glued together just yesterday, for all I knew.

My stirring, puzzling first glimpse into sophistication's toy shop prepared the way for many subsequent visits when, between August of 1955 and April of 1957, I found myself a citizen of New York, working ten short blocks to the south of West Fifty-third Street. I walked here often, up Fifth Avenue, to clear my head, to lift my spirits. For me the Museum of Modern Art was a temple where I might refresh my own sense of artistic purpose, though my medium had become words. What made this impu-

GEORGES BRAQUE
Woman with a Mandolin, 1937
Oil on canvas, 51 1/4 × 38 1/4"
The Museum of Modern Art, New York. Mrs. Simon Guggenheim Fund

dent array of color and form Art was the mystery; what made it Modern was obvious, and was the same force that made me modern: time. Indeed, some of the works that arrested me—Picasso's *Girl before a Mirror*, its ice-creamy colors and fat satisfied black outlines posed in those days at the turning of the main stairs; Rouault's *Christ Mocked by Soldiers*, with its outlines of a coarser sort framing colors passionate as raw meat; Giacometti's *Woman with Her Throat Cut*, so amusingly lobsterlike a bronze of such a dreadful subject—dated from 1932 and were thus just my age, which seems to me now very young. In those days Abstract Expressionism was becoming the great imperial art, the internationally stunning emblem of American daring and power. But, though there may have been a Pollock or Rothko or two already on the walls, to a relatively unsophisticated museumgoer like me semi-abstract, semi-comic allusive paintings such as William Baziotes' cyclopean green *Dwarf* and Jean Dubuffet's astonishingly rough-textured *The Cow with the Subtile Nose*

(Left) PABLO PICASSO
Girl before a Mirror, 1932
Oil on canvas, 64 × 51¹/₄″
The Museum of Modern Art,
New York. Mrs. Simon
Guggenheim Fund
© 2000 Estate of Pablo Picasso/
Artists Rights Society (ARS),
New York

(Right) GEORGES ROUAULT
Christ Mocked by Soldiers, 1932
Oil on canvas, 36¹/₄ × 28¹/₂″
The Museum of Modern Art,
New York. Given anonymously

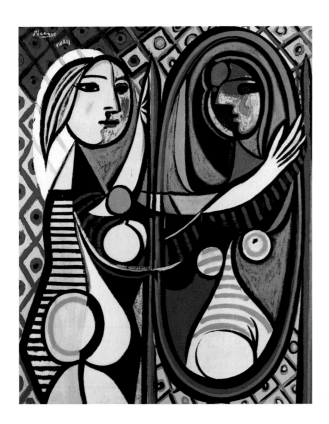

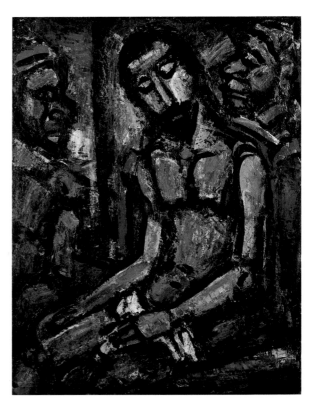

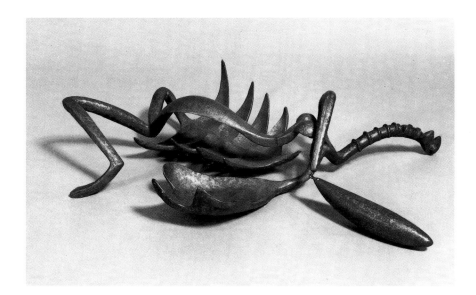

ALBERTO GIACOMETTI
*Woman with Her
Throat Cut*, 1932
Bronze (cast 1949),
8 × 34 1/2 × 25″
Collection, The Museum of
Modern Art, New York.
Purchase

were as modern as paintings could get. I naïvely expected paintings to have titles, and seriously pondered the enamelled details of anecdotal, illustrational canvases like Pavel Tchelitchew's *Hide-and-Seek* and Peter Blume's *The Eternal City,* with Mussolini as a jack-in-the-box. I was young enough to find delight, still, in allusions to toys, like the toy car that forms the mother baboon's head in Picasso's *Baboon and Young,* and the bicycle handlebars that make the horns in his *Goat Skull and Bottle.*

But it was among the older and least "modern" works in the museum that I found most comfort, and the message I needed: that even though God and human majesty, as represented in the icons and triptychs and tedious panoramic canvases of older museums, had evaporated, beauty was still left, beauty amid our ruins, a beauty curiously pure, a blank uncaused beauty that signified only itself. Cézanne's *Pines and Rocks,* for instance, fascinated me, because its subject—these few pine trunks, these outcroppings of patchily tinted rock—was so obscurely deserving, compared with the traditional fruits of his still lifes, or Mont Sainte-Victoire, or his portrait subjects and nude bathers. The *ardor* of Cézanne's painting shone most clearly through this curiously quiet piece of landscape, which he might have chosen by setting his easel down almost anywhere. In this canvas, his numerous little decisions as to tone and color impart an excited shimmer to the areas where the green of the pines shows against the

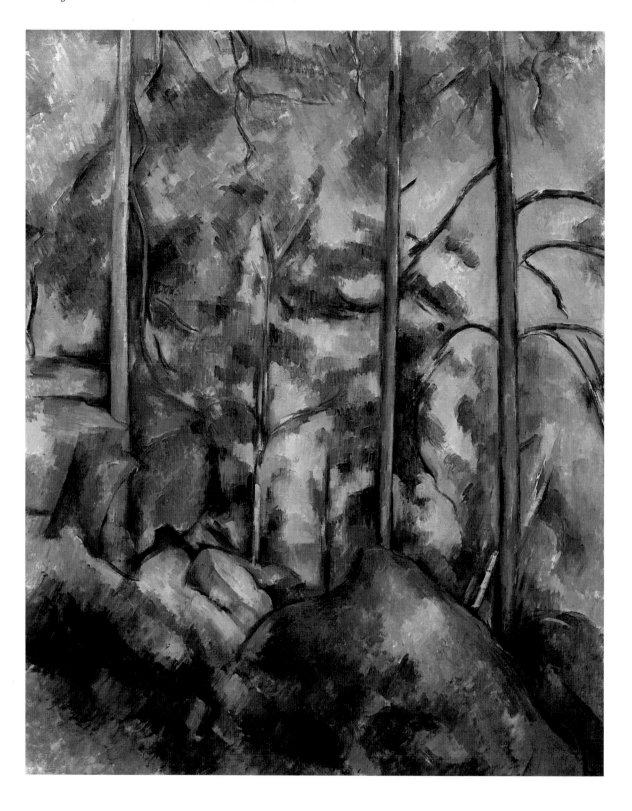

blue of the sky, to the parts of the ochre trunks where shadow and outline intermix, and to the foreground, rendered in parallel diagonal strokes, of earth and grass. Blue, green, and ochre—these basic shades never bore him, and are observed and captured each time as if afresh. In the intensity of the attention they receive, the painter's subjects shed their materiality: the pines' branches here and there leap free of the trunks, and the rocks have no heaviness, their planes all but dissolved in the rapid shift of grayish-blue tints. What did it mean, this oddly airy severity, this tremor in the face of the mundane? It meant that the world, even in such drab constituents as pines and rocks, was infinitely rewarding of observation, and that simplicity was composed of many little plenitudes, or small, firm arrivals—paint pondered but then applied with a certain nervous speed. Cézanne's extreme concentration breaks through into a feeling as carefree and unencumbered as that which surrounds us in nature itself. In its new, minimal frame, *Pines and Rocks* seems smaller than the canvas I remember from the Fifties—but the grandeur of its silence, the gravity with which it seems to turn away from the viewer toward some horizon of contemplation, is undiminished.

The Matisses, too, attracted me with their enigmatic solemnity. Hardly monochromatic, yet usually with some strong single scrubbing of fundamental color—the red of the *Red Studio,* the gray of *Piano Lesson,* the dull pink of *The Rose Marble Table*—they expressed not so much a fanatic observation of nature as a blithe domination of it. Such freedom! How impudently, in *Piano Lesson,* does the painter take a wedge from the boy's round face, flip it over, and make of it a great green obelisk, barely explicable as a slice of lawn seen through a French door! I knew of nothing so arbitrary in writing—a regal whimsy enforced by the largeness of the painting, whose green was already cracking and aging in another kind of serene disregard. The little boy, but for the cruel wedge laid across his eye, looked normal to me, but the other figures—the little brown nude, the tall unfinished figure merging with her chair—were, I realize now, emissaries from another world: they were art twice over, representations of Matisse works already distributed in this domestic space. *Red Studio* even more baldly reduced an interior to the art it contained— the furniture mere outlines, only the paintings painted. From this painting of paintings, in a setting flattened to a single red color, it was not a great step to abstract canvases of pure paint, whose only subject was their own execution. Of course, Matisse's simplifications, though I have described

PAUL CEZANNE
Pines and Rocks, 1896–99
Oil on canvas, 32 × 25 3/4"
The Museum of Modern Art,
New York. Lillie P. Bliss
Collection

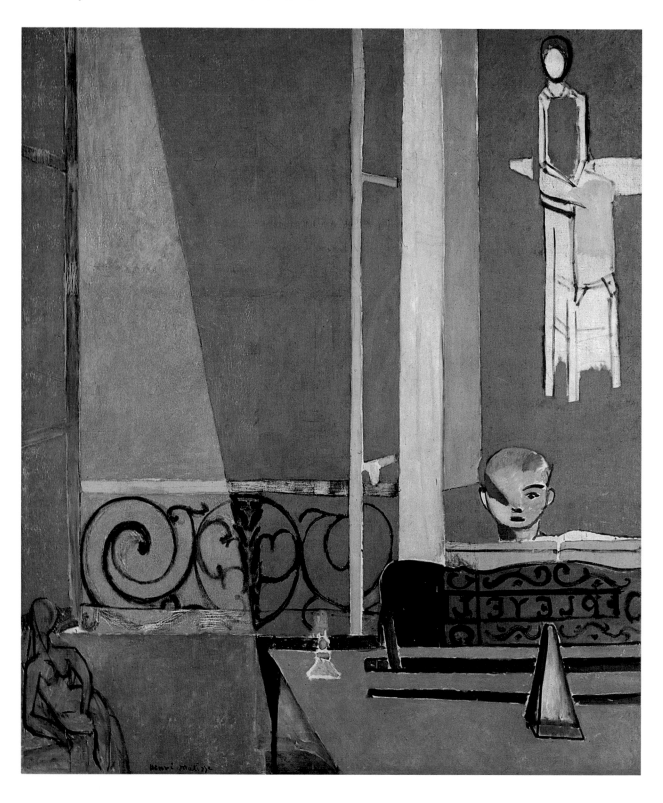

them in terms of violence, made (unlike Picasso's) an impression of benevolence and peace, and his flowers, his fruits, his goldfish, his nudes seemed elements of an artists' Eden, located in a France of perpetual soft summer, where nothing was necessary but to eat and sleep and see.

This old-fashioned idea of mine that art should body forth the idyllic found confirmation in many corners of the museum. Its exhibition chambers, after all, formed a soothing shelter from the streets outside, which, though less so than those same streets now, were even then overtrafficked and clamorous. The immense windows rimmed in rounded dark metal sealed the taxi tops and bouncing heads of Fifty-third Street into an aquarium hush, and in the other direction one could look over the high wall of the sculpture garden at the windows of a caramel-colored apartment building where, supposedly, Elizabeth Taylor lived, among others almost equally rich and famous. The paved garden, before it made room

(Opposite)
HENRI MATISSE
Piano Lesson, 1916
Oil on canvas, 8′ ¹/₂″ × 6′ 11³/₄″
© 2000 Succession H. Matisse, Paris/Artists Rights Society (ARS), New York

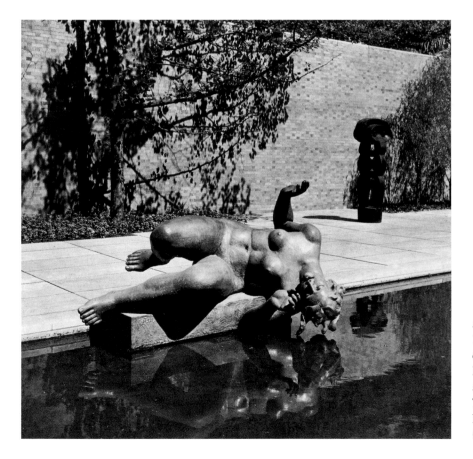

ARISTIDE MAILLOL
The River, begun 1938–39, completed 1943
Lead, 53³/₄″ × 7′ 6″,
at base 67 × 27³/₄″
The Museum of Modern Art, New York. Mrs. Simon Guggenheim Fund

for the welded constructions of David Smith and Anthony Caro, was a quiescent glade of basically female forms—Renoir's *Washerwoman* squatting to her task, Maillol's lead-pale nude *River* trailing her hair in the little pond, Lachaise's *Floating Figure* and *Standing Woman* flaunting their naked hyperfemininity, Matisse's series of mute broad backs lining the wall, Moore's seated *Family Group,* and, for touches of playfulness, Nadelman's little graceful bronze figure with the bowler hat and Picasso's *She-Goat* with her emphatic udders and vulva.

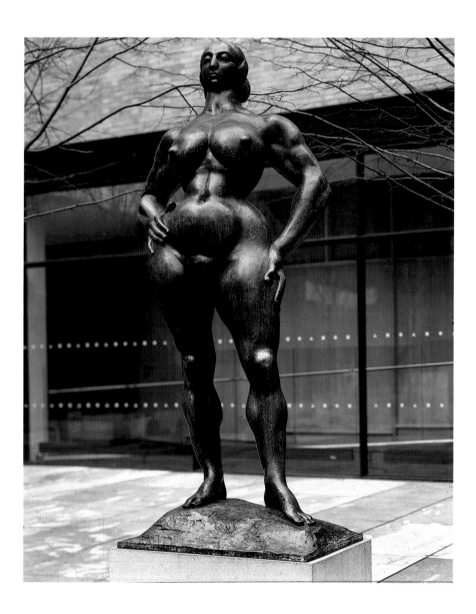

GASTON LACHAISE
Standing Woman, 1932
Bronze, 7′4″ × 41¹/₈ × 19¹/₈″
The Museum of Modern Art,
New York. Mrs. Simon
Guggenheim Fund

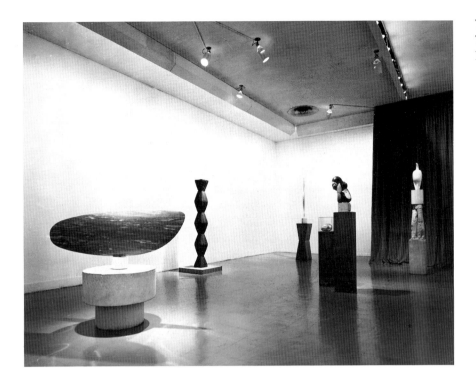

The Brancusi room, in 1954
The Museum of Modern Art,
New York

Within the museum, Brancusi's statues were grouped in a corner room (not in a walk-through gallery as now), and emanated an extraordinary peace and finality — the floating *Fish* of gray marble whose stratifications became events in an imagined water, the soaring *Bird in Space* of polished bronze that etherealized the viewer into an elongate reflection, the carved wooden *Cock* like an upside-down staircase, the innocent egg-shapes of *Young Bird* and *Mademoiselle Pogany* resting her head on her hands, and the white marble *Maiastra* mounted at a height suitable for manifesting a goddess. These pet shapes (there may also have been an *Endless Column* and a *Blonde Negress* in the group) had acquired, in the decades of the sculptor's obsessed reworking of them, a sacred aura, which I imbibed as in a chapel, in that softly lit corner space from which one could only turn and retreat.

I was looking for a religion, as a way of hanging on to my old one, in those years, and was attracted to those artists who seemed to me as single-minded and selfless as saints:

> Brancusi, an anchorite
> among rough shapes,

blessed each with his eyes
until like grapes
they popped, releasing
kernels of motion
as patiently worked
as if by the ocean.

Cézanne, grave man,
pondered the scene
and saw it with passion
as orange and green,
and weighted his strokes
with days of decision,
and founded on apples
theologies of vision.

Picasso seemed a bit too noisy, too bustling and carnal, for my hagiology, but there was a painting by fellow Spaniard and Cubist Juan Gris which I often contemplated with reverence. *Breakfast,* though a less sunny and matinal work than Bonnard's *The Breakfast Room,* tastes more like breakfast: a stark but heartening outlay of brown coffee and thick white china, with a packet of mail and piece of newspaper at its edges. The yellowing scrap of jOURNal, which wittily includes the artist's name in headline type, fascinated me: like the cracked green of Matisse's *Piano Lesson,* the scrap was showing the chemical effects of time; it was aging away from the white of the tablecloth toward the grained brown of the table. On the table, the impudent yet somehow earnest use of commercial paper imitating wood-grain moved me, echoing here in this palace of high art the kitschy textures of my childhood exercises in artifice; and the perfect balance and clarity of this crayonned collage, together with the short life testified to by Gris's dates on the frame (1887–1927), exuded the religious overtone I sought. A religion reassembled from the fragments of our daily life, in an atmosphere of gaiety and diligence: this was what I found in the Museum of Modern Art, where others might have found completely different—darker and wilder—things. Gaiety, diligence, and freedom, a freedom from old constraints of perspective and subject matter, a freedom to embrace and memorialize the world anew, a fearless freedom drenched in light: this was what I took away, each time, from my visits of an hour or so, usually in the afternoons, my day's journalism done, before heading south to my wife and apartment and daughter on

JUAN GRIS
Breakfast, 1914
Pasted paper, crayon, and oil
on canvas, 31 7/8 × 23 1/2″
The Museum of Modern Art,
New York. Acquired through
the Lillie P. Bliss Bequest

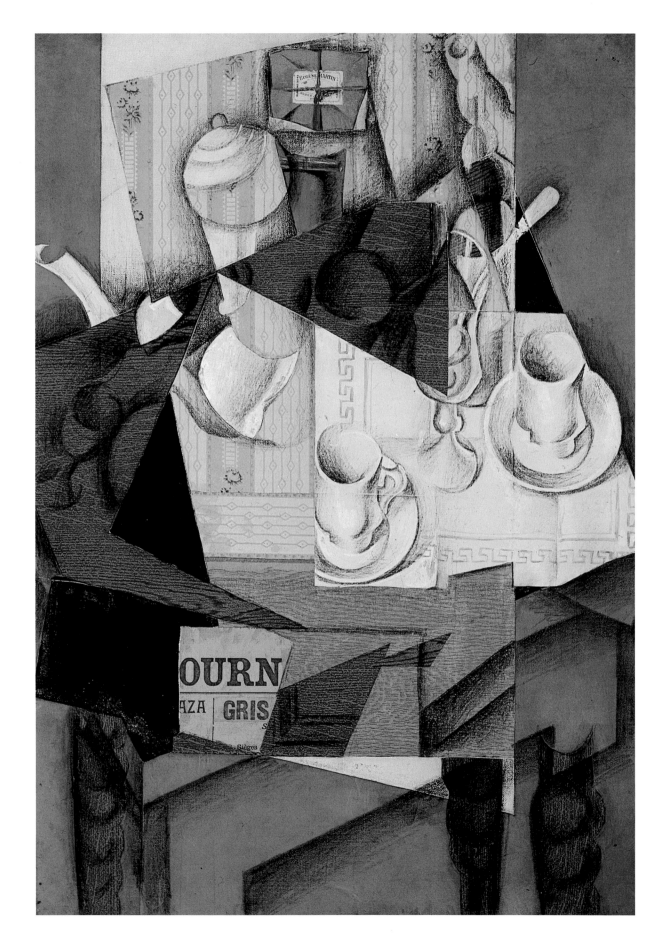

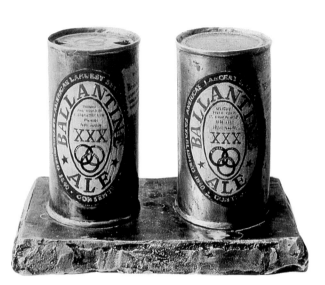

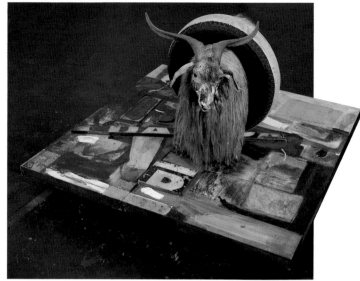

(Left) JASPER JOHNS
Painted Bronze, 1960
$4^3/_4 \times 5^1/_2 \times 8''$
Leo Castelli Gallery, New York

(Right) ROBERT RAUSCHENBERG
Monogram, 1963
Freestanding combine,
$42 \times 64 \times 64^1/_2''$
Moderna Musset, Stockholm

West Thirteenth Street. I took away, in sufficient-sized packets, courage to be an artist, an artist now, amid the gritty crushed grays of this desperately living city, a bringer of light and order and color, a singer of existence.

I moved to New England, yet often returned, a visitor now among the swelling tourist crowd, yet still a marveller, as the old masterpieces of modernity underwent an occasional shuffle in the exhibition rooms, supplemented as they were by ever bigger and prouder abstractions, and then by the grim hilarities of Pop—Rauschenberg goats and spattered assemblages, Warhol silk screens and stacked Brillo boxes—and by Jasper Johns' neoclassical targets and flags and maps and beer cans and Robert Indiana's stately lettering and Lichtenstein's comic strips and Op Art's dazzling brief parade of vibrating stripes and spots. Op was the last art movement I enjoyed, and Minimalism the last one I was aware of; I could not adjust to artworks that lay on the floor, bricks and tiles and coils of ropes that could be accidentally kicked. Outside the museum, on Fifty-third Street and beyond, the world changed, becoming experimental to the point where nothing art could do seemed revolutionary or subversive in the way that Pollock's drip paintings and de Kooning's hectically brushed portraits of women had seemed in the gray flannel world of the Fifties. Life in the Sixties and Seventies, and not merely painting, had become expressionistic performance. And the Japanese and Germans and Vietnamese and Saudis were cutting America down to size, and the art world was swamped by money bloat and by national tired blood.

Irrationally, I felt betrayed when Picasso's *Guernica,* which had for so long greeted visitors to MoMA's second floor, was returned to a suddenly democratic Spain, and again when, as part of a plan to cash in on the condominium boom with yet another midtown high-rise, the museum's exhibition space was doubled, making it one more museum too big to wander through without getting backache. When does modern end? It began, MoMA says in its own literature, "about 1885"; over a century has gone by, and the dignified course might be for the museum to declare itself a closed treasury, like the Cloisters and the Frick. But it has opted, instead, for a greedy open-endedness and a bigger souvenir shop; it has led the transformation of museums into gorgeous tourist traps, where once they were sober and even torpid enhancements of local civic life. The steepleless cathedral of artistic faith I used to visit is still there, but as a box within boxes, its message diffused and its relics scrambled. The last time I walked through, I couldn't find my favorite Gris, or *Hide-and-Seek,* or *The Eternal City,* or Arp's *Mountain, Table, Anchors, Navel,* or that construction of paper and string that long ago had looked to my childish eyes like a kite preserved in an attic.

My youthful visits, pious, joyful, and ignorant, inspired a love and nurtured a strange confidence that has emboldened me, from time to time, to write on the visual arts. I have reviewed a few shows for *The New Republic,* composed a book review or essay upon occasion, and for a stretch did a series of five-hundred-word essays under the head of "Impressions" for a doomed but cheerful American version of the French art magazine *Réalités.* To make a book's worth I have added this reminiscence and my researches into two artists who intrigued me, Ralph Barton and Jean Ipoustéguy. These writings are the fruit of just looking, of the pleasures of the eye, which of all our sensory pleasures are the most varied and constant and, for modern man, the most spiritually pliable, the most susceptible to that sublimation called, in pre-modern times, beauty. That beauty and its fanatic pursuit persist even into the attenuated metaphysical ruin of the twentieth century is, I suppose, the overriding lesson I absorbed, when young, in the Museum of Modern Art.

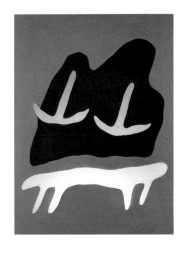

Jean Arp
Mountain, Table, Anchors, Navel, 1925
Oil on cardboard with cutouts, 29⅝ × 23½″
Collection, The Museum of Modern Art, New York. Purchase

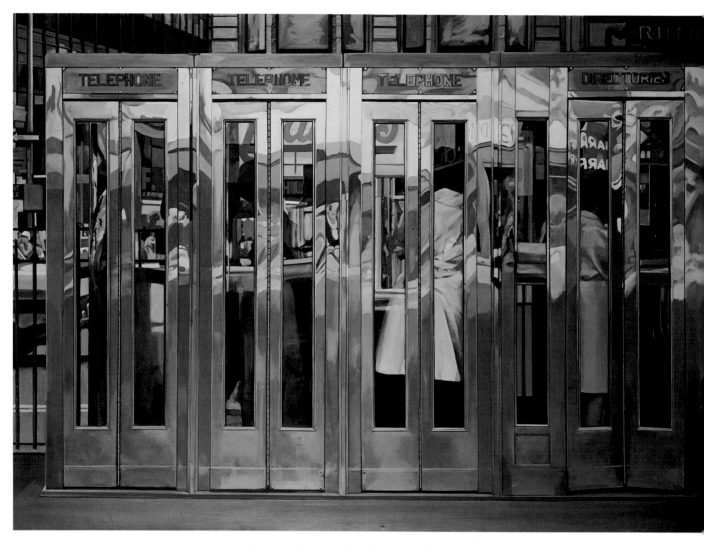

RICHARD ESTES   *Telephone Booths*, 1968. Oil on canvas, 48×69″
© Museo Thyssen-Bornemisza, Madrid

A City Frieze

NOBODY LOVES our hideous city streets as Richard Estes does. Upon the aluminum surfaces of these inflexibly aligned booths he has found any number of patches of color as luminous and independently gemlike as the "little patch of yellow wall" that Proust's alter ego Bergotte found in Vermeer's *View of Delft*. Estes usually works with deeper perspectives—depopulated avenues, dizzying vortices of advertising and architecture—and this shimmering frieze stops us short. Which booth is free? We look closer. All are taken.

The perspective is deeper than it first appears. One side of the street shows above and through the booths, and the other, at our back, is reflected, liquefied by minute waves in the mirroring metal strips. An abundance of urban activity crowds the thin margin around the solemn rectangular silence of the booths. The sun is shining on a car hood. A fat woman is striding past a mannequin. Merchants are proclaiming their names and wares in visual shouts reduced to isolated letters—an alphabet flung about as recklessly as children's blocks.

How hard it is to hear at a public telephone! Slices of life slide past the smudged windows, previous standees have left disagreeable spoor, the eyes and ears receive entirely different worlds: a kind of trick is being played upon reality that makes us want to laugh, though the voice at the far end of the connection, speaking out of its own welter of distractions, has sad or self-important news. No wonder these doors are closed so snugly, all but the one on the right, where a tiny triangle of air gives vent to an implied claustrophobia. No wonder they have their backs to us, these callers, shutting us out as well in their attempts to focus, to keep hold of their threads of conversation amid the garish clutter that presses on all sides.

Estes, like the cities that are his subject, feasts the eye to surfeit. His paintings would be unendurable but for their merciful eclipses. We know nothing of the two people on the right but their light clothes. Of the pair on the left we know even less; they appear transparent in the swim of reflections. By the etiquette of metropolitan crowding their persons have been reduced to mere signifiers that the booths are taken; like computer bytes or slugs of type, they fill their slots and give the information. The bleakness of this information, contrasted with the richness of the visual information the painter has unstintingly imparted, makes for an utterly tender artistic irony. Daylight, unnoticed, reaches down into the urban gloom and whitens the top of each booth.

Straining to hear, sealed with their urgent privacies into identical gleaming cells, the four faceless callers themselves receive the attention of the painter, who renders with the coolly sensuous touch of a Vermeer what hitherto would have seemed too ugly to paint, too dreary to see. And behind his shoulder we stand, locked into his curious peace, simultaneously attentive to his art and face to face with our environment.

An Outdoor Vermeer

—————

ONCE I vowed to see every Vermeer hanging in a public museum throughout the world, and did in time stand before many of them. There are fewer
than forty authenticated paintings by this Dutch master, and the best of
them are perhaps the loveliest objects that exist on canvas. They tended, it
seemed to me in the course of my pilgrimage, to come in pairs—for instance, the two dashing, heavily pointillist, oddly behatted female heads
in the National Gallery of Art in Washington (*Girl with a Red Hat, Girl
with a Flute*) and the two cool, bluish, satin-clad, askance-glancing young
women at virginals in London's National Gallery (*Lady Standing at the
Virginals, Lady Seated at the Virginals*). *The Lace-Maker* in the Louvre
startled me by being so small, and *View of Delft,* hanging in the ill-lit
Mauritshuis in The Hague, surprised me by being so large—over a yard
high and nearly four feet wide. I was taken unawares by its breadth, its
depth, its palpable *plein air.* Most Vermeers are less than half this size, and
only three find their subject matter out of doors.

Delft is where Jan Vermeer was born, in 1632, lived, and died, in 1675.
He was buried in the Old Church, which shows here as the tower on the
left. The New Church, in sunlight on the right, stood diagonally across
from Vermeer's house on the market square at the center of the town. It is
strange to think that just outside those windows that admit light to the
enchanted still spaces of Vermeer's domestic paintings the bustle of a main

square daily resounded, and that other rooms of the same house, which was called Mechelen, held a tavern. Vermeer had inherited the tavern and an art dealer's business from his father, Raynier Janszoon, who began calling himself van der Meer or Vermeer when his son, christened Johannes, was about twenty. At this same age of twenty Jan married a local girl, Catharine Bolnes, by whom he had eleven children. He was a member and twice chairman of the Guild of Saint Luke, the artists' guild. He supported himself and his immense family not by his own painting but by dealing in the paintings of others; on one recorded occasion he helped adjudicate a dispute between the Elector of Brandenburg and an Amsterdam art dealer and decreed that the paintings in question "did not deserve to bear the name of a good master." The financial records Jan left indicate a frugal life, and three years before he died the Vermeers rented Mechelen and its tavern to a tenant and moved to a smaller house. His sole bequest to his widow was between thirty and forty of his paintings. She struggled to save at least some of them from their creditors. Two were used to settle a baker's bill, and twenty-one were auctioned off in Amsterdam in 1696, and thence passed from owner to owner in the following centuries for less, ordinarily, than the price of a suit of clothes.

Little more is known about Vermeer. As in the case of Shakespeare, biography is dumb, and the art speaks the louder for that. *View of Delft* is listed in the 1696 auction catalogue and is signed, too faintly to be seen in reproduction, on the boat on the left. The time of its painting is estimated to be 1660, at the outset of Vermeer's miraculous prime. He must have achieved his view from the second floor of a house across the River Schie; it has been speculated that the painter, who may well have used the viewing device known as the *camera obscura,* turned the entire room of his vantage into such a camera by closing the shutters on all but a small, lenslike hole. Vermeer's exact contemporary and the receiver of his estate was Anton van Leeuwenhoek, the inventor of microscopy. The photographic perspective of many of Vermeer's scenes and the sparkling presence of those flattened dots of paint called *pointilles* (here conspicuous on the boat seams and the gable edges) strongly suggest that he did use some optical aids.

But it is a human vision that shapes this magnificent townscape—spacious yet intimate, intense yet exquisitely balanced. Many of the buildings still stand, and it can be seen that Vermeer moved them about for aesthetic effect. And it was a human hand that laid on the paint with such

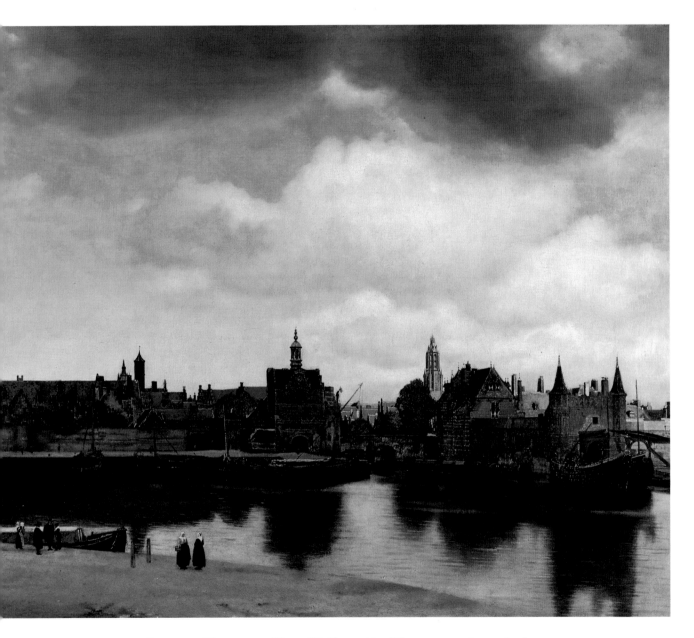

JOHANNES VERMEER   *View of Delft*, c. 1660. Oil on canvas, 38³/₄×46¹/₄″
Mauritshuis, The Hague

infallible precision, in four distinct bands of elemental texture. The canvas is half sky, and an atmosphere more monumentally vaporous has never been rendered. Rain is potential in the topmost clouds while light soaks through to the crisp city spread below. Golden sun strikes some buildings while others wait in shadow; the earth is thus related to the "in and out" sky and the whole scene given a strong momentum: an instant of flux forever held. Proust thought this "the most beautiful painting in the world," and his character Bergotte dies while contemplating its *petit pan de mur si bien peint en jaune"*—a detail difficult to identify among the several yellow patches on the left, flanking the Rotterdam Gate. The brick buildings in their somber warm colors crackle with *pointilles* like the bread in the foreground of *Maidservant Pouring Milk*—a painting also attributed to 1660, and like *View of Delft* a virtual symbol of Holland. Vermeer at this moment of his development, already rendering optical sensations with a fidelity that would not be appreciated until the era of photography and Impressionism two hundred years later, has not yet arrived at the almost inhuman coolness of his later work and allows his subjects a dignity and interest that is partly theirs, that does not derive solely from the magic of his painting.

Beneath the crusty, active, charming breadth of Delft itself runs a strip of surpassingly liquid, shadowy river, and tucked diagonally beneath that is a foreground of sand that looks raw and featureless by comparison. Indeed, I remember leaning forward, while I beheld *View of Delft* in the dusky Mauritshuis, to be sure that this rough swatch of ochre was not a piece of damage that the painting had suffered in its travels, or an unfinished corner such as one finds in Cézanne. But no, it is painted, and it is here, on this little lip of wilderness in canalled and cobbled Holland, that Vermeer has situated his human figures, like voyagers sent to the moon from the neatly crammed world across the Schie. The painter in his interiors often appositely hung a map or an allegorical figure above the heads of his women as they dreamily test a balance, read letters, or muse over music. There was a symbolizing tendency in him that here seems to pose these citizens in their prim black and white beneath the glistening walls and pinnacles of Delft like a maker's signature: they, from their bank of sand, made this. Just so—the artist seems to announce in the virtuoso textures of this, his consummate and only landscape—he, Jan Vermeer, could paint anything.

The Apple's Fresh Weight

ADAM AND EVE occupy a huge but peculiar place in Judeo-Christian mythology. Responsible for man's fall, and for all the suffering and evil consequent, they are yet regarded with affection, and always have been. Their story as told in Genesis is one of the most vivid and humanly engaging in either Testament. In *The Divine Comedy*, Dante, having assigned two high-minded assassins of Caesar to the lowest realm of Hell, locates Adam in the seventh heaven of Paradise, and receives from him an amiable lesson in semantics. Milton in *Paradise Lost* pities but scarcely blames the erring pair, and gives them a beautiful dignity as they consort on sociable terms with angels. Something primordial overrules morality in their case; they are the parents of us all, and like children perennially we are free to indulge and mock but not to condemn. Their great begetting places their case above judgment, and gives it something of the cosmic good humor credited to tough old Mother Earth herself.

In the history of art, Adam and Eve performed a special service: via their bodies the nude figure was transported from Greece and Rome through the Dark Ages into a safe niche within Christian iconography. A late-Roman ivory diptych shows Adam reclining in flaccid but utter nakedness, penis and fleece and all, as lord of animal creation; on the bronze doors of Hildesheim, in the early eleventh century, Adam and Eve, looking like marionettes with barrel chests and stick limbs, clutch to their

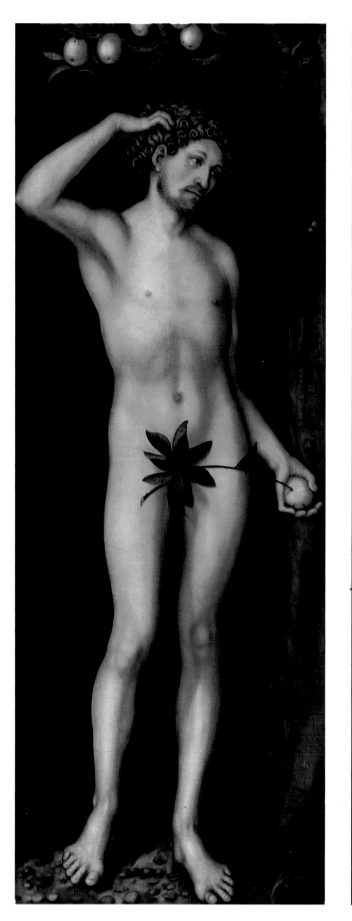
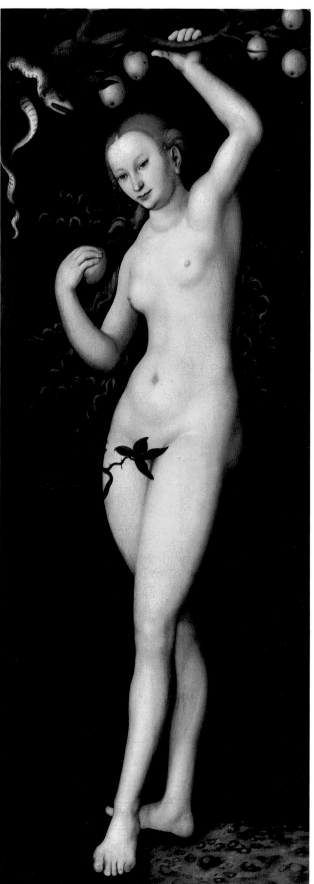

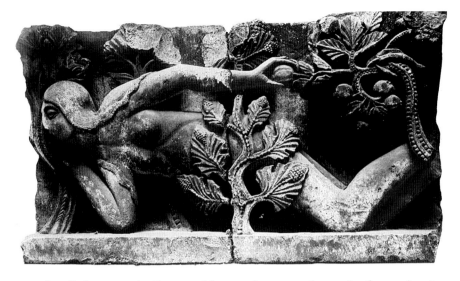

GISLEBERTUS
Eve, c. 1150
Sculptural relief on north
transept portal,
Cathédral St. Lazare
Musée Rolin, Autun, France

crotches fig leaves as bulky as cabbages. A century later, the first seductive female nude in Christian art appears on a door lintel at Autun Cathedral, an Eve gliding among the leaves of Eden like a snake, plucking the forbidden fruit while her eyes gaze ahead in dreamy, abandoned reverie.

Lucas Cranach's Eve is also somewhat snakelike—a snake with a seductively luminous skin. What an erotic apparition she is! Her soft apple-sized breasts are pulled upward into the same tilt as her slitted eyes. Her orange hair explodes behind her in corkscrews of energy. Adam's hair, too, is curly; his fingers explore it in this initial moment of male puzzlement. Eve's hand, in contrast, clings to the same limb where her mentor, the serpent, entwines in ominous echo of her own flexible radiance. She has shaved thoroughly, a fact ill-concealed by the leaves that a branchlet extends with a deference we might fancy ironical. No bathing-suit tan has ever striped this woman's skin; the hardened and airbrushed nakedness flaunted in countless twentieth-century centerfolds cannot recover her immaculate, sumptuous pallor. The Gothic nude, in Kenneth Clark's phrase, was "dragged out of the protective darkness in which the human body had lain muffled for a thousand years." Eve's face wears an Oriental calm brought from beyond the rim of Christendom. Adam's legs could come from a crucifix; yet his abdomen is unscarred and presents, like Eve's, a tender frontal challenge. Flesh is delicious. We gaze here upon the primal scene—the parents of us all when young, desirous, their hands curved about the apple's fresh weight. Lost Eden still hangs above their heads; the stony earth of the future lies at their feet. Between, the naked present shines.

(Opposite)
LUCAS CRANACH, THE ELDER
(Left) *Adam,* c. 1530
Oil on panel, $75 \times 27^{1}/_{2}''$
Norton Simon Art Foundation,
Pasadena

(Right) *Eve,* c. 1530
Oil on panel, $75 \times 27^{1}/_{2}''$
Norton Simon Art Foundation,
Pasadena

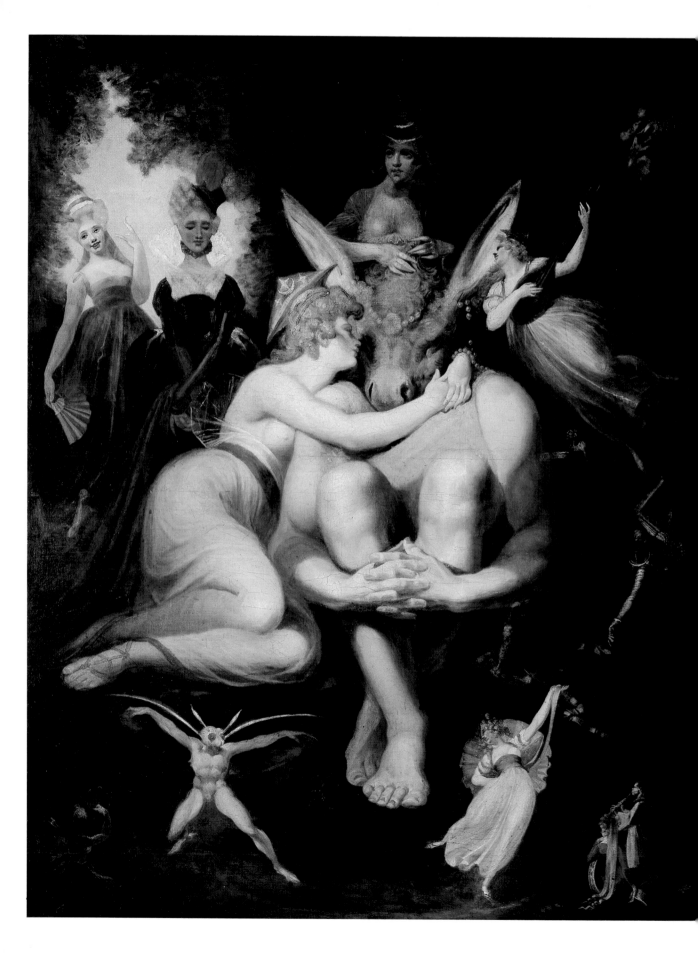

A Case of Overestimation

———

THE BRITISH PAINTER John Henry Fuseli—born in Zurich, an early sur-
realist, an encourager of William Blake—here poses the problem of scale,
in an appropriate erotic context. Changing size is exciting, whether preg-
nancy, tumescence, or simple organic growth is the cause. I once had a
young daughter who could not bear to look at that Tenniel illustration in
which Alice's neck elongates, it was so exciting to her. I myself as a child
was subject, before falling asleep, to sensations of strange hugeness, in
which entire galaxies could be encompassed within my thumb. And when
we arrive at mating age we are excited by differences in size — feminine
petiteness/masculine bulk are the common match, but the terms can be
reversed, with potent comic effects, as with the stately chorus girl and the
scampering little comedian, all drooping suspenders and gaga eyes. The
ovum looms above the wriggling spermatozoon.

   Here, framed in the deluding darkness of a midsummer's night, Bully
Bottom is a creature out of human scale, his frame enlarged and thickened
to support his ass's head. Beside him Titania appears of a smaller order,
though hefty in hip and breast. Imagine her hands in his. The fairy between his ears, perhaps Peaseblossom ("Scratch my head, Peaseblossom"—Act IV, Scene i), and the two ladies on the left, surely Helena and
Hermia, belong to a third order of size, and the fairy with the lute to a
fourth. Those at the bottom of the canvas, let us say Moth and dainty

JOHN HENRY FUSELI
(Johann Heinrich Füssli)
Titania and Bottom
(*Titania liebkost Zettel mit
dem Eselskopf*), 1793–94
Oil on canvas, 66 1/2 × 53″
Kunsthaus Zürich, Switzerland
Vereinigung Zürcher
Kunstfreunde

Cobweb, are smaller still, and in the righthand corner two musicians scarcely bigger than a signature introduce yet another degree of diminution, a sixth. For a seventh, possibly Mustardseed, the fourth of Titania's serving-fairies, exists microscopically somewhere in Fuseli's teeming chiaroscuro.

One trouble with theatrical productions of *A Midsummer Night's Dream* is that all actors are human, and the fairies therefore must clumsily bulk in the same scale as Theseus and Hippolyta, who ideally should be ten feet tall. A hierarchy of stature should prevail—from rulers to gentry to commoners, and then from the rulers of the fairy kingdom down through their subjects and most delicate minions. Putting children into bit parts, or casting Mickey Rooney as Puck, scarcely mitigates the violence done to the subtle gradations that Shakespeare's words establish on the page. With flashlights and cumbersome cardboard props the actors must carry out Titania's exquisite injunction:

> The honey-bags steal from the humble bees,
> And for night-tapers crop their waxen thighs,
> And light them at the fiery glowworm's eyes,
> To have my love to bed, and to arise;
> And pluck the wings from painted butterflies,
> To fan the moonbeams from his sleeping eyes.

In her infatuation she speaks great poetry, as fine in its music as Juliet's and Cleopatra's. No skillful stage carpentry can make good, as her enraptured words do, her promise to her beloved monster:

> And I will purge thy mortal grossness so
> That thou shalt like an airy spirit go.

Would that love *could* purge mortal grossness. Titania's embarrassing situation is the more poignant for being typical: every morning of the world, men and women awaken from the dream of infatuation, to exclaim with her same bleak wonder, "Methought I was enamoured of an ass!"

"Overestimation of the sexual object" was Freud's formula for the discrepancy of scale that breeds love. Eros thrives on difference, on otherness. Small, we love what is big, or vice versa; queens love monsters; the weave of delusion hums underneath and overhead; and the body and the spirit never quite fit.

The Child Within

SUSAN E. MEYER, the author and assembler of the luxurious *America's Great Illustrators* and *Norman Rockwell's People,* has now produced, less luxurious but still a posh enough album, *A Treasury of the Great Children's Book Illustrators*—thirteen in number, all born in the nineteenth century, and each represented by about a dozen samples of their work and a dozen big pages of biography. She begins with Edward Lear and ends with W. W. Denslow, the illustrator of *The Wizard of Oz* (but of none of the other Oz books, which went on merrily without him and eventually without L. Frank Baum, their creator). In between we have John Tenniel, a *Punch* cartoonist who against the author's best instincts (Lewis Carroll liked his *own* illustrations) enhanced the two Alice books; Walter Crane and Randolph Caldecott, the twin giants of the Victorian "toy-book" industry captained by the printer Edmund Evans; Kate Greenaway and Beatrix Potter, shy spinsters (as soon as Miss Potter married, she ceased to write and draw for publication) whose dainty art enchanted vast audiences; Ernest H. Shepard, another *Punch* cartoonist who became involved with a set of children's classics, in his case the four Christopher Robin books by A. A. Milne; Arthur Rackham, who like Shepard took a whack at *The Wind in the Willows* and like Tenniel at *Alice in Wonderland;* Edmund Dulac and Kay Nielsen, who along with Rackham prospered during the vogue for deluxe gift books that died out after World War I;

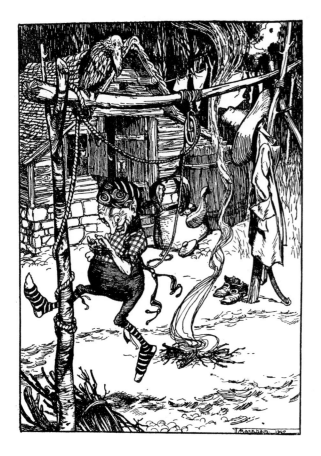

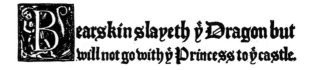

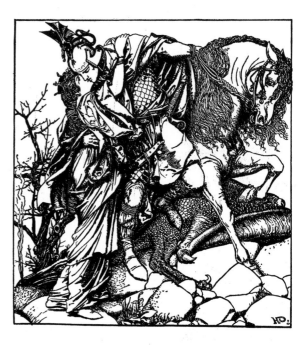

(Left) ARTHUR RACKHAM
From "Rumpelstiltskin" in
Grimm's Fairy Tales (1909)
Ink drawing reproduced by
wood engraving

(Right) HOWARD PYLE
From *The Wonder Clock* (1888)
Ink drawing reproduced by
wood engraving

and Howard Pyle and N. C. Wyeth, one the founder and the other the most formidable product of the "Brandywine school" of illustration, which at last put Americans in the forefront of the genre.

Children's-book illustrations are among the first art objects we gaze upon; it is strange, then, that so many are gloomy and frightening. I can remember being, if not quite terrified, certainly depressed by the spidery, brownish, gnarled drawings in the books with which I was supposed to pass my feverish convalescences in bed. The stink of the dead past emanated from these leering gnomes and wooden princesses; death nested in every crabbed detail. In Ms. Meyer's *Treasury*, the plates by Rackham and Pyle and Crane especially still wear for me this dreary power. A child is alive on a newly made island of time. What he or she usually wants for reassurance is the indubitably contemporary—not cobwebbed gargoyles from never-never land but cheerful puppets from an unsullied *now*. For me, the cheap Disney comic books, with their plump buttony furniture and rubber-legged quasi-animals, conjured up a fantasy world I could enter without fear of being trapped in a crypt of the unfathomably long ago.

The famous, and brilliant, illustrations Tenniel created for the two Alice books pose a special problem of dread. I found the deep crosshatching and the angry playing cards menacing, but with nothing of the morbid fascination that afflicted my younger daughter when she was, perhaps, six. The drawing, specifically, of Alice elongating made her squeal with an emotion I could only, at a wild guess, relate to the phallic suggestion of the stretched neck and its startled small head. Once, experimenting, I offered to peek with my little girl at this potent illustration, and at the moment of vision she cried out and slapped the book shut so furiously the forbidden page was torn in half.

The world, let us say, is full of scary things, and it is children's-book illustrations that first offer to display them to us. The amount of emotion, for example, that at some early point I myself invested in those exquisite little watercolors Beatrix Potter painted for her *Peter Rabbit*—particularly the one wherein Peter, exhausted and caught in the gooseberry net, "gave himself up for lost, and shed big tears"—is surely disproportionate, considering that in the next instant "his sobs were overheard by some friendly sparrows, who flew to him in great excitement, and implored him to exert himself," and that then, so encouraged, he extricated himself by

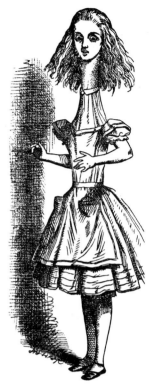

JOHN TENNIEL
From *Alice's Adventures in Wonderland* (1865)
Ink drawing reproduced by wood engraving

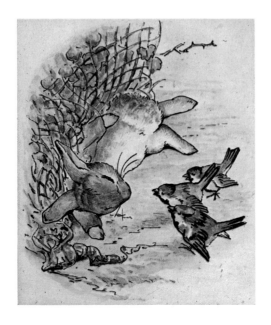

BEATRIX POTTER
Illustration from *The Tale of Peter Rabbit* (1902)
Watercolor
Copyright © Frederick Warne & Co., 1902, 1987. / Reproduced by kind permission of Frederick Warne & Co.

the expedient of shedding his new blue jacket. The pathos of the drawing, and of the one previous, showing him caught in the gooseberry net, lay to my childish sense somehow in the visual fact that in both pictures Peter is *upside down*—as a parent or God would see a sleeping child while standing at the head of the bed. The illustrator of children's books surpasses all other artists in the impressionability of his audience; what touches will produce an indelible effect is beyond calculation, no doubt, the receiving surface of a child's psyche being so soft and mysteriously laden and momentous with its own raw energy.

To my adult vision the freshest of these "great" illustrations are by Lear, Caldecott, Potter, Shepard, and Wyeth. Those by Nielsen and, to a lesser extent, by Dulac have a Beardsleyesque creepiness and static elegance that must always have appealed more to fine-book collectors than to childish perusers. The case of Kate Greenaway is a curious one; her melancholy furbelowed little maidens were once the rage of England and goaded John Ruskin to ecstasies of stricture and praise, in the voluminous correspondence he and Greenaway continued for nine years. "I could contentedly and proudly keep you drawing nice girls in blue sashes with soft eyes and blissful lips, to the end of—my poor bit of life," he wrote her, and solemnly told an Oxford audience, "In her drawings you have the radiance and innocence of reinstated infant divinity showered again among the flowers of English meadows." The daughter of a milliner and a wood engraver, Greenaway derived her quaint costumes from those seen in an old-fashioned village, called Rolleston, where she had been sent as a girl;

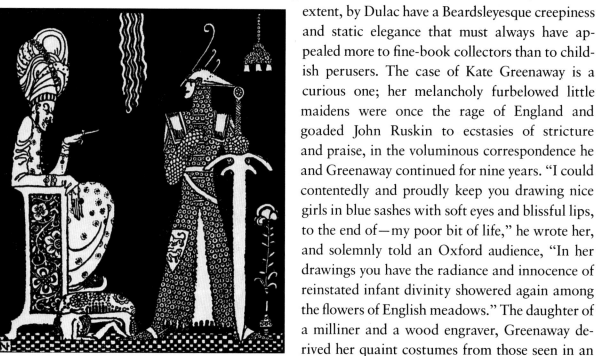

KAY NIELSEN
From *East of the Sun and West of the Moon,* by P. C. Asbjørnsen, (1914). Ink drawing reproduced by wood engraving

her wispy, wistful art seems to be one of those secret messages that nations send themselves, a murmur of lost English innocence that was well received, too, on this side of the Atlantic. Potter's appeal rested, contrariwise, on a certain solid realism; she and her brother used to skin, dismember, and draw small creatures, and accordingly her animals have fur and claws, muscles and aroma.

The history of children's-book illustration cannot be separated from the history of book production, and Ms. Meyer traces the progress from

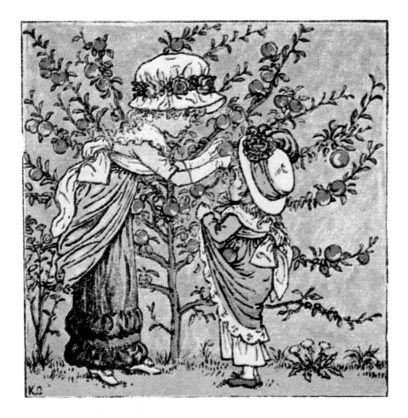

KATE GREENAWAY
From *Kate Greenaway's
Birthday Book* (1880)
Ink drawing reproduced by
wood engraving

wood engraving for black-and-white reproduction to the first clumsy color overlays, and thence to the development of photogravure, which by the century's end had pretty well eliminated the artist's laborious collaborator, the painstaking chiseller of blocks of boxwood. Tenniel depended heavily upon the judgment and skill of his engravers, Joseph Swain and the Brothers Dalziel, who signed the blocks for the Alice books with their names as well as Tenniel's monogram. Walter Crane began his career in an engraver's shop, and in his *Reminiscences* described the round night-work table "with a gaslamp in the centre, surrounded with a circle of large clear glass globes filled with water to magnify the light and concentrate it on the blocks upon which the engravers (or 'peckers' or 'wood-peckers,' as they were commonly called) worked, resting them upon small circular leather bags or cushions filled with sand, upon which they could easily be held and turned about by the left hand while being worked upon with the tool in the right."

The woodcut look helped give Tenniel's illustrations their pleasing crispness; Crane made an artistic virtue of necessity by emphasizing the full thick outlines and two-dimensional patterns the medium favored. "Children," he said, "don't want to bother about three dimensions. They can accept symbolic representations. They themselves employ drawing . . . as a kind of picture-writing." A disciple of Morris and a keen socialist, Crane anticipated the Soviet style and those illustrators, such as Denslow and Rockwell Kent, who cultivated the woodcut look for its own decorative sake. Edward Lear, oddly, drew as if for twentieth-century photogravure, freely and sketchily and plainly in penstrokes. Caldecott, too, had a calligraphic fluidity—favoring a brown outline to a black—and Evans created for him superimposed engravings that approached the delicacy of watercolors. As the photographic methods of color separation and the corresponding control of inking improved, artists could entrust ever-richer effects to the technicians. Rackham, as if to forestall the murk of reproduction, worked in murky blurred tones of his own, but Dulac dared the brilliance of Persian miniatures, and N. C. Wyeth simply painted big oil canvases to serve, much reduced, as book illustrations. His palette and impasto were an old master's, and his work joins the mainstream of American easel painting.

Ms. Meyer's biographical sketches lead us deftly through lives on the whole tame and tranquil. Some of her details surprise us: Shepard served four years of combat in World War I, and Tenniel at the age of twenty was blinded in one eye while fencing. Both artists, however, lived productively into their nineties. Only Dulac, who was interested in the occult, and Denslow, who had a drinking problem, seem at all bohemian. Both the women were childless, as were Tenniel, Caldecott, Dulac, Lear, and Nielsen. As Ms. Meyer says, "the child within" is the one that matters for this sort of communicator.

Lear, Potter, and Greenaway were their own writers—or, if you prefer, their own illustrators. The majority illustrated fairy tales and adventure stories that others had written. The three notable cases of a living collaboration—Tenniel and Lewis Carroll, Shepard and Milne, and Denslow and Baum—produced amicable marriages of picture and text but on the personal level no great cordiality: Milne and Lewis Carroll were jealous of the degree to which the illustrators' images had captivated the public mind, and Denslow, after collaborating closely with Baum in the day-to-day creation of Oz, split with him over credits and the division of

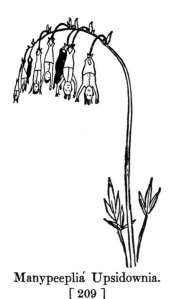

Manypeeplia Upsidownia.
[209]

EDWARD LEAR
"Manypeeplia Upsidownia"
from *Nonsense Songs, Stories, Botany, and Alphabets* (1871)
Ink drawing reproduced by
wood engraving

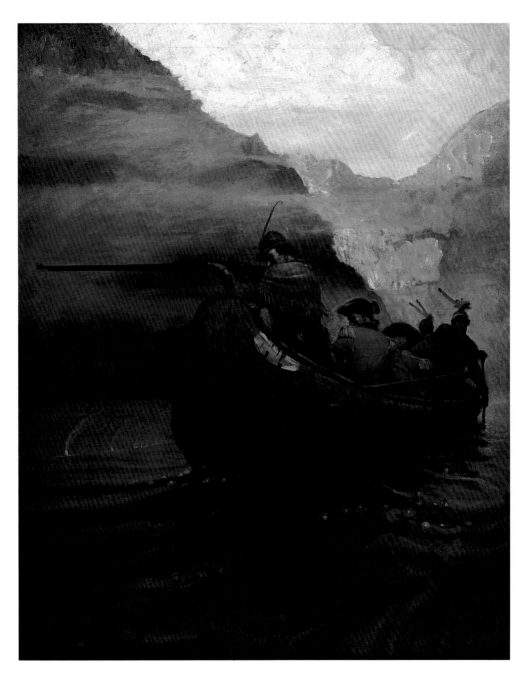

N. C. WYETH *The Flight Across the Lake.* Oil on canvas, 40 × 32 ¹/₄″
Used as illustration for *The Last of the Mohicans* (1919)

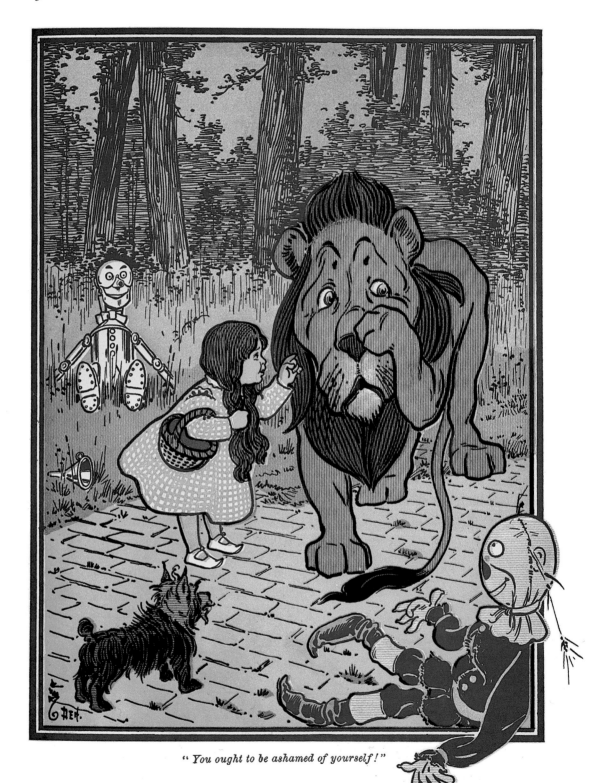

"*You ought to be ashamed of yourself!*"

earnings. There was a great deal of quarrelling, indeed, in the history of children's books as writer, illustrator, and publisher jockeyed for their share of the proceeds of this enterprise—an enterprise born of the industrial revolution not only in the evolving printing technology but in the emergence of children as a consumer class.

(Opposite) W. W. DENSLOW "You ought to be ashamed of yourself!" from *The Wizard of Oz,* by L. Frank Baum (1900) Ink drawing reproduced by photoengraving, with mechanical color halftones

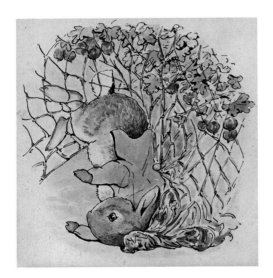

BEATRIX POTTER Illustration from *The Tale of Peter Rabbit* (1902) Watercolor Copyright © Frederick Warne & Co., 1902, 1987. / Reproduced by kind permission of Frederick Warne & Co.

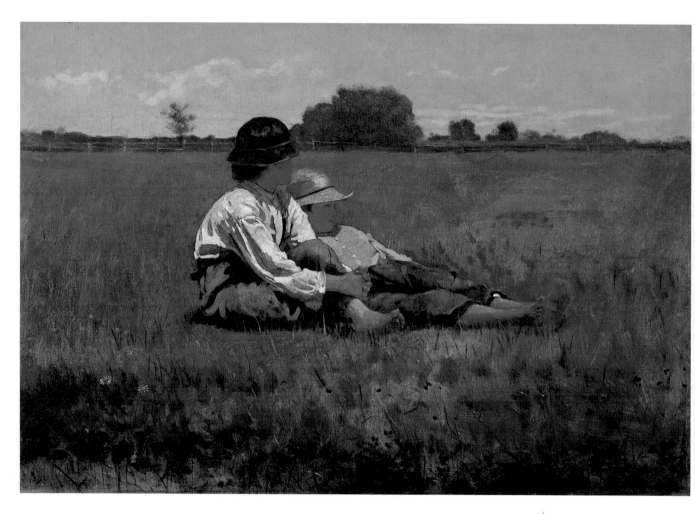

WINSLOW HOMER   *Boys in a Pasture*, 1874. Oil on canvas, $15\frac{1}{4} \times 22\frac{1}{2}''$
Museum of Fine Arts, Boston. The Hayden Collection

American Children

THE BOYS and girls depicted here might not mix very well if they were released from their frames, but separately they compose two peaceful groups and two beautiful paintings. Winslow Homer's anonymous lads are taking their ease in a pasture; the daughters of the prosperous Edward Boit are scattered through two fine rooms, and all but one of them gaze with respectful curiosity at the busy bearded intruder into their home, the fashionable painter John Singer Sargent. The dashing impressionism of Sargent's technique carries a generation farther Homer's flickering grasses and dabs of sunny red, and the triangular pose of the little girl in the foreground mirrors the unified shape of the two country idlers. Both painters surround their childish subjects with large margins of environment. The effect is of silence: silent vases, silent sky, silent carpet and turf underfoot. A great hushed world waits around these children to be tasted, explored, grown into.

They take themselves seriously, and are taken seriously. Homer gives his little subjects a monumental dignity; there is something of Greek drapery in the color-gouged fold of the sunlit white sleeve, and something angelically graceful in the extended, self-shadowed feet. And Sargent, catching his subjects where they have alighted like white butterflies, displays deep spaces about them, and permits them all the gravity their young femininity warrants. They recede, from youngest to oldest, toward

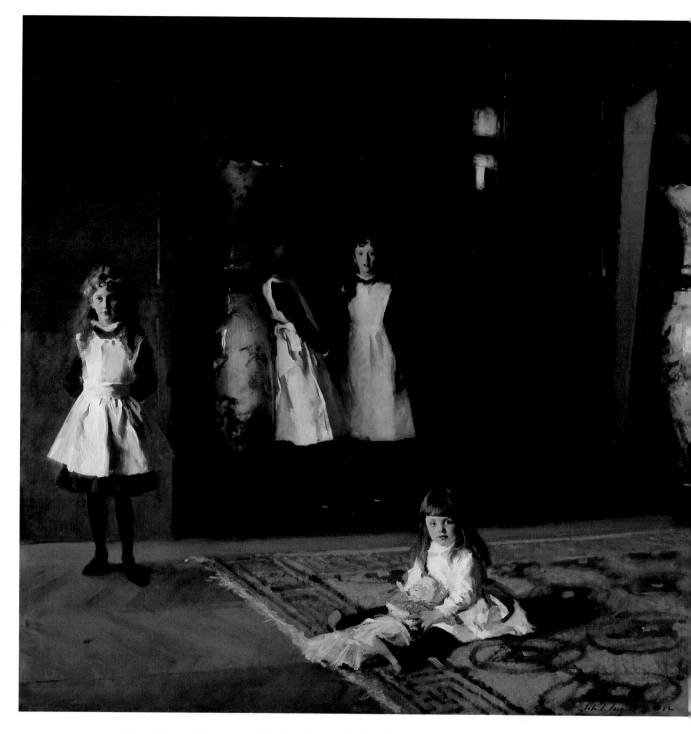

JOHN SINGER SARGENT   *The Daughters of Edward D. Boit,* 1882. Oil on canvas, 87×87″
Museum of Fine Arts, Boston. Gift of Mary Louisa Boit, Florence D. Boit,
Jane Hubbard Boit, and Julia Overing Boit, in memory of their father, Edward D. Boit

a dark other room; beyond the toddler with her doll a girl no longer quite childish stands on the edge of shadow while her sister, a little taller and older still, is half-turned into it. The huge vase she leans against suggests a woman's shape. These young ladies are watching, not just the painter, but us, to see what we will do next, and whether what we do will be worthy of their responding. Like butterflies, they will elude us if we startle them.

Sargent's painting could have been a mere commission, an expert piece of toadying within the upper classes, but the jaunty eccentricity of its composition, and a daring within its deference, save it for art. Winslow Homer's could have been a bit of calendar art, falsely bucolic, but for the abstract power of a severe and stately composition that locks the barefoot pair as if forever into the center of the canvas and that lends solemn substance to a fleeting summer day. There is a mystery to the faces; the painter has declined all opportunity for easy anecdote within the ruddy shade of those hats.

Both artists have attempted honest portraits of children, as perhaps only Americans could have done. Though the Declaration of Independence nowhere promises a better deal for children, the American child does appear freer than his European counterpart and is taken more seriously—as a source of opinion, as a market for sales, and as not just a future inheritor but an independent entity now, while still a child. Childhood and then youth are seen in our democracy as classes that cut across class distinctions. Within their frames these two sets of children are similarly pensive. Responsible but powerless, childhood does not smile; it watches and waits, amid shadows and sun.

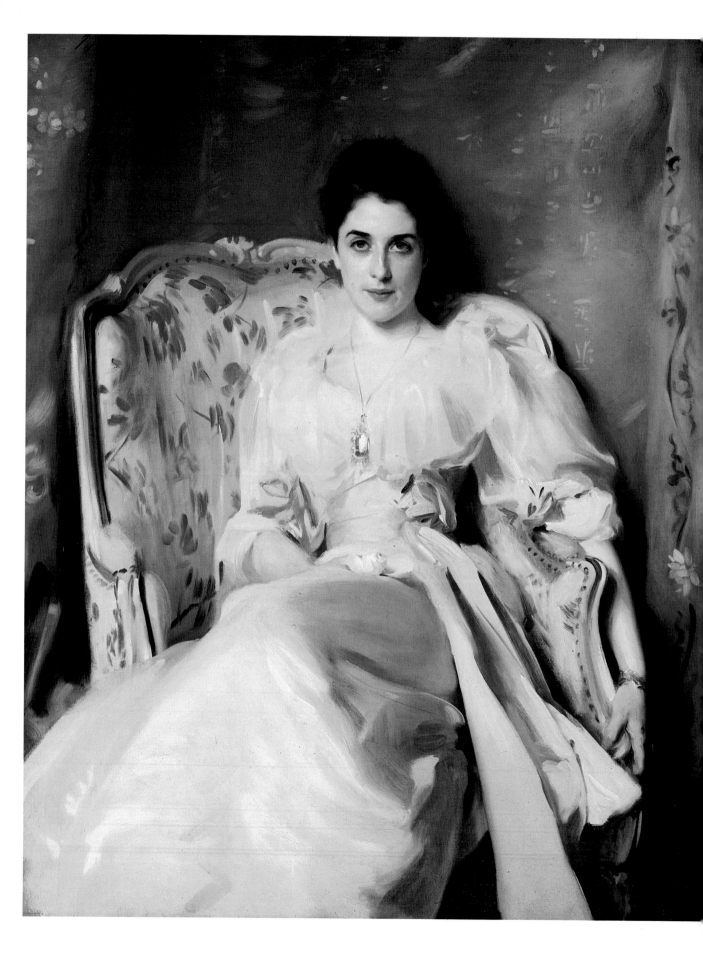

Something Missing

———

AMERICANS like in their artists a touch of the hermit crank, of the ascetic; Homer and Hopper had it, and Eakins and Pollock. But not John Singer Sargent: he was too facile, too successful, too professional, too European. The most fashionable of artists in his portrait-painting prime from 1887 to 1907, he turned to murals as a path to higher realms and instead covered his name with a certain polite dust. His death in 1925 (like his life, apparently painless) prompted two large retrospective shows the following year, at the Royal Academy in London and the Metropolitan Museum in New York, but no tribute as generous has been launched for sixty years; now, in the fall of 1986, the Whitney Museum of American Art has mounted an impressive yet faintly melancholy exhibit in New York. The show is not apt to change people's minds about Sargent, or to secure him a place higher than his present honorable position as the creator of some spectacular canvases yet a man who, in the statement formed by his total career, somehow misses. "Yes," Henry James wrote to Thomas Bailey Aldrich in 1888, "I have always thought Sargent a great painter. He would be greater still if he had one or two little things he hasn't—but he will do."

He did do, for his times, and did handsomely for himself in that happy age of weekend grouse shoots and wood-panelled steamship staterooms, and will do for the lines of helpless megashow addicts who curl around

JOHN SINGER SARGENT
Lady Agnew of Lochnaw,
c. 1892–93
Oil on canvas, 49 × 39¹⁄₄″
The National Gallery of
Scotland, Edinburgh

the corner of Madison and Seventy-sixth; but what *were* those little things? We go to the retrospective as if to the sickbed of a very dear and charming friend whose debilitating illness still, distressingly but also rather amusingly, eludes diagnosis. We stand in front of the paintings waiting for something to happen and wondering why it doesn't, and wondering what it would be if it did. The brushstrokes are dashing, the pictorial wit is unfailing, the presence of the subjects in the strongest works, the portraits, is at times astounding. It was a frequent criticism of Sargent, even as his triumphs and fees mounted, that his portraits lacked psychological depth—not a quality, perhaps, that the sitters were paying for. But in fact who could be more *there,* as a living, gazing presence, than Lady Agnew of Lochnaw, seductively slumped in her white dress and looking out with a contemplative challenge from beneath her dark brows and darker hair, or her companion on the wall (and friend in life) Miss Helen Dunham, nervously glancing away while clasping her pink hands in her lap? The sumptuous wealth of stuffs—long dresses, velvet hangings, flowered furniture—in the society portraits detracts from the intelligent intensity with which the faces are rendered. Elizabeth Swinton sat—stood, really—for a portrait that, meant to be her wedding present, was finished barely in time for her second anniversary; her flushed complexion and plump, bruised-looking lips perhaps show her impatience with the painter as (she reported) he "wasted a lot of time" singing and banging on the piano; but these ripe and unsmiling lips also show the qualities that may have led the affable if asexual Sargent to dally and flirt. A woman of a much less peachy type, Mrs. Charles Thursby, is posed in dark brown, in a seated position of pronounced tension, as if she is about to leap up past the painter and mount a horse sidesaddle; her level green eyes, rendered with great care, come forward, and her mouth is daringly (for the mouth is the key to likeness) left sketched in paint, a brilliant blurred suggestion. With equal daring, Catherine Vlasto's brow and eyes are left in shadow while the light falls on her neck and right side and the hand that oddly flattens several keys of the piano she leans against. These women, if not psychoanalyzed as Rembrandt and Velázquez and even Copley psychoanalyzed some of their sitters, are not cheaply beautified either, and are present as enigmatically and undeniably as real people in a room.

Where female vanity and the pomp of the full-length pose were not involved, Sargent exploited without inhibition the knowledge of the human face that his hundreds—more than eight hundred, it is thought—of por-

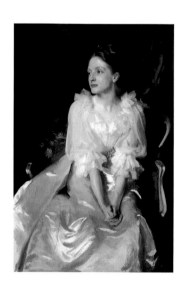

SARGENT
Miss Helen Dunham, 1892
Oil on canvas, 48 1/2 × 32 1/2″
Courtesy of Vance Jordan Fine Art, Inc.

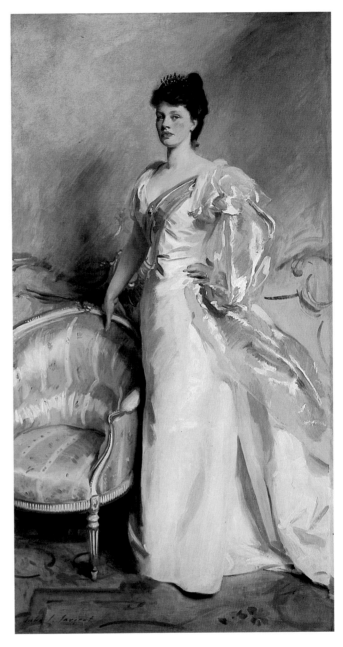

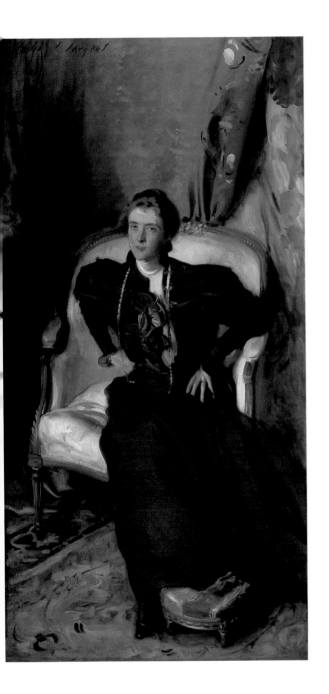

SARGENT
(Above) *Mrs. George Swinton*, 1896. Oil on canvas, 90 × 49″
The Art Institute of Chicago
Potter Palmer and Wirt D. Walker Funds

(Left) *Mrs. Charles Thursby*, 1897–98. Oil on canvas, 78 × 39³/₄″
Collection of The Newark Museum, New Jersey

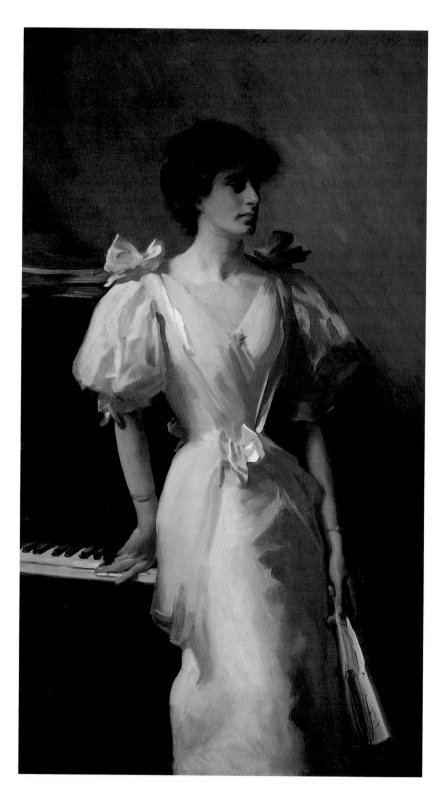

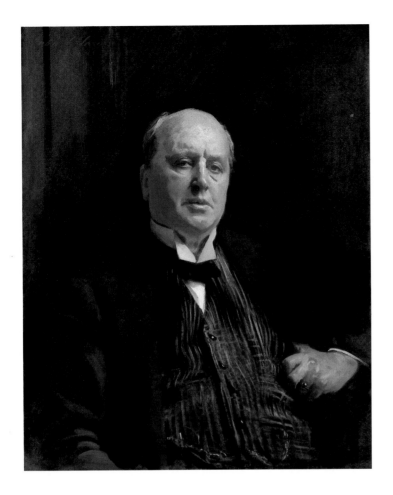

SARGENT
Henry James, 1913
Oil on canvas, 33 1/2 × 26 1/2″
By courtesy of the National
Portrait Gallery, London

traits had earned for him. He has left the definitive painted images of Henry James, his friend, admirer (with James's usual shrewd reservations), and twin Anglo-American star in London society; the portrait head displayed at the Whitney delicately reveals an oppressive puffiness about James—a leaden watchful intelligence in the eyes, a domineering mouth partly open as if to resume an endless stream of calculated utterance. The handsome, dramatically shadowed charcoal image of Yeats that the poet commissioned for the frontispiece of his first collected poems is also definitive, and arresting. Sargent's little hasty heads of friends, especially that of Charles Stuart Forbes, do penetrate into personality, and the swaddled visage of a Bedouin Arab painted during a trip to Egypt in 1890–91 has a staring force. The artist's sexual activities and proclivities

(Opposite) SARGENT
Catherine Vlasto, 1897
Oil on canvas, 58 1/2 × 33 3/4″
Hirshhorn Museum and
Sculpture Garden, Smithsonian
Institution, Washington, D.C.
Gift of Joseph H.
Hirshhorn, 1972

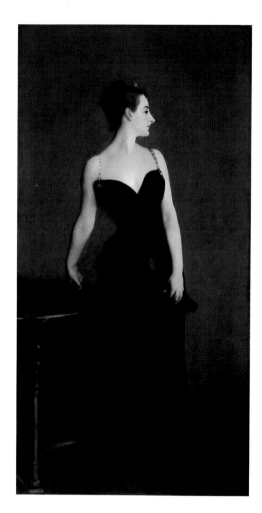

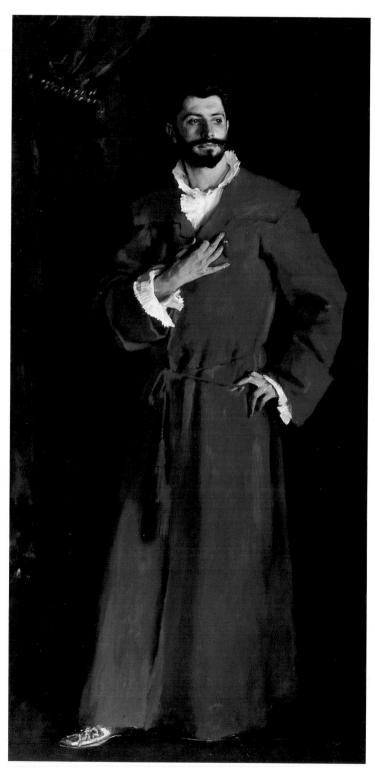

SARGENT
(Above) *Madame X*
(Madame Pierre Gautreau), 1884
Oil on canvas, 82¹/₈ × 43¹/₄″
The Metropolitan Museum of Art, New York
A. H. Hearn Fund

(Right) *Dr. Pozzi at Home,* 1881
Oil on canvas, 80¹/₂ × 43⁷/₈″
The Armand Hammer Collection,
UCLA Hammer Museum

have not excited any very lively interest among his biographers, but the men of his portraits, generally, seem more in danger of idealization than the women. Compare the notorious portrait of Madame X (Madame Pierre Gautreau) with its companion-piece, the portrait of her rumored lover, Dr. Pozzi: the former is so icy and angular and lurid a vision of aspiring glamour that Paris howled and the subject declared herself ruined, while the latter is shameless romantic flattery of its bright-eyed subject, with a cozy crimson aura of satanic drag.

Sargent had an underindulged instinct for the marginal; in Venice, he painted not gondolas but working girls in their dark factory-palazzos, and among his commissioned portraits those of wealthy Jews are strikingly vital. The (to my eye) rather stiff and sickly portrait of Mrs. Carl Meyer and her children was greatly admired when displayed, converting even Sargent-doubters to his praise: Henry Adams crustily wrote, "The art of portrait-painting Jewesses and their children may be varied but cannot be further perfected." The two canvases at the Whitney of the Wertheimer family are so warm and engaging as to seem anomalous—the pair of sisters physically linked with an intimacy more expectable in a mother and daughter, and the genial sly face of Asher Wertheimer, an art dealer and a patron of Sargent's, glowing at us out of deep chiaroscuro like a patriarch by Rembrandt. This painting of Wertheimer tells us what we have been missing in even the more admirable of Sargent's portraits:

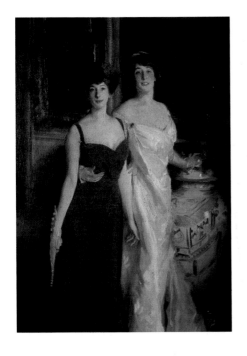 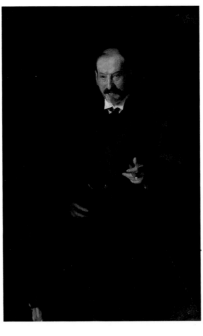

SARGENT
(Left) *Ena and Betty, Daughters of Mr. and Mrs. Wertheimer,* 1901
Oil on canvas, 73 × 51 1/2"
The Tate Gallery, London

(Right) *Asher Wertheimer,* 1898
Oil on canvas, 58 × 38 1/2"
The Tate Gallery, London

an at-ease emotional possession of the subject that enables him to concentrate on making a painting. Where no warming familiarity exists, a certain distancing finesse takes over. The ivory skin and turquoise gown of Millicent, Duchess of Sutherland, repel the eye, as hauteur should, though she is showing even more décolletage than the scandalous Madame X; Sargent has flattened Marlborough's Arcadian backgrounds to a mere backdrop, a stage set for a fearsomely lovely Titania. The painter's performance is so consummate as to be self-mocking, and the elongation of the body is unreal.

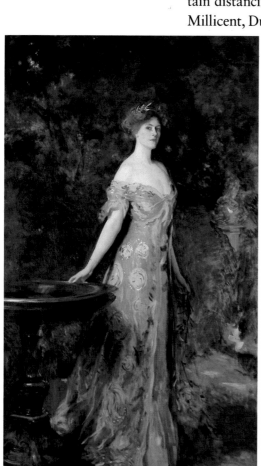

SARGENT
Millicent, Duchess of
Sutherland, 1904
Oil on canvas, 100 × 57½"
Copyright © Museo Thyssen-
Bornemisza, Madrid

It would take a larger cross-section than the Whitney provides to test my suspicion that Sargent made better portraits of Americans, expatriate or not, than of the English upper classes. But it is hard to imagine an English couple inspiring (or paying for) a canvas as jaunty and sporty as that of Mr. and Mrs. I. N. Phelps Stokes, of New York. Anecdotes about the painting have been preserved. The Stokeses, newly married, were visiting London. Mrs. Stokes was originally intended to pose wearing a green evening-dress, with her hand resting on the head of a Great Dane. One day she came into Sargent's Tite Street studio wearing a summery starched linen skirt and blue serge jacket, and he asked her to pose in that; where her hand had been extended to rest on the dog's head a boater hat appeared on her hip, and her husband, ghostly in a white suit, materialized behind her. Such cheerful improvisations were Sargent's native bent, but after the scandal of the Madame X portrait drove him from Paris to London, he curbed his picture-making fancy for the business of what he came scornfully to call "paughtraits." The portraits of his that get into art books came early—that of Madame X in 1884, and the casually original and affecting group of the four Boit daughters in 1882. By contrast, the group of the three Vickers sisters done in Sheffield two years later is a studied and unsteady effort; each face is pursued in a different style, and the surrounding dark space is incoherent.

Nothing, however, prevented him, rich on commissions, from spending summers doing subject paintings out of doors, in his version of the Impressionist manner. Monet, whom he knew and even painted beside, re-

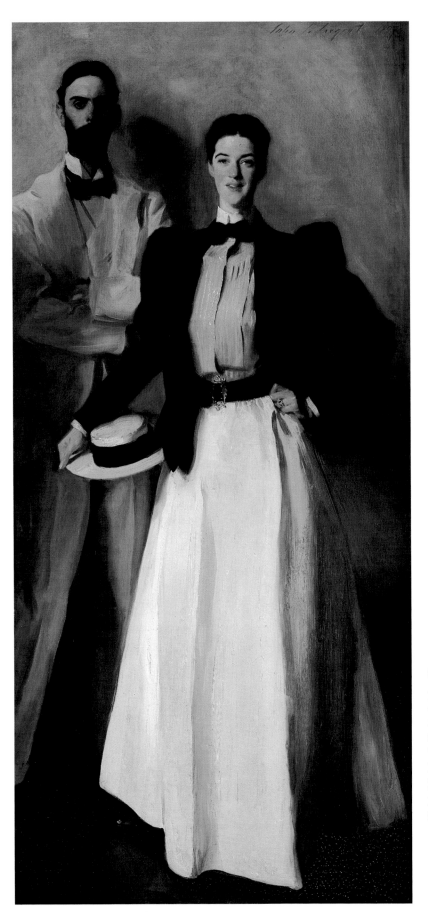

SARGENT
Mr. and Mrs. Isaac Newton Phelps Stokes, 1897. Oil on canvas, $85 1/4 \times 39 3/4''$
The Metropolitan Museum of Art, New York. Bequest of Edith Minturn Phelps Stokes (Mrs. I. N.), 1938

SARGENT
Carnation, Lily, Lily,
Rose, 1885–86
Oil on canvas, 68½ × 60½"
The Tate Gallery, London

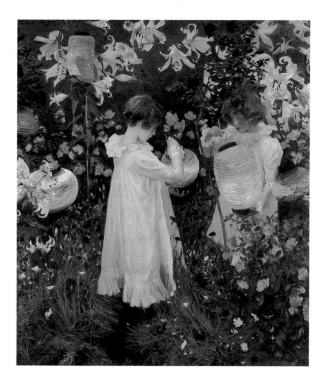

counted that once Sargent borrowed his palette and was appalled to find no black on it. "How do you do it?" he asked the French master. His own first loyalties, learned from his Parisian teacher Carolus-Duran, were to the Spanish darks of Velázquez and to the darting, flippant brushwork of Frans Hals. His famous canvas *Carnation, Lily, Lily, Rose* (not in the Whitney show) was credited with bringing, in 1886, Impressionism to England and did evince at least the Impressionist fidelity to atmospherics, having been painted by Sargent in twenty-minute snatches through the twilight of two summers; but he was only popularly viewed as an Impressionist, and his works along the lines of Monet and Renoir are, by and large, not only weak but ugly. His inability to let go of black and brown shadows gives his outdoor scenes a dour look; they seem much older than the 1880s and '90s, when they were painted. On the other hand, a relatively bright and unmuddy effort like *Millet's Garden* seems crude, in composition and brushwork both. *Garden Study of the Vickers Children,* though something of a breakthrough for him, has, on its dull-green ground, the artificial flatness, lifted from Japanese prints, of fin-de-siècle magazine illustration. Green, perhaps, was not Sargent's best color; he

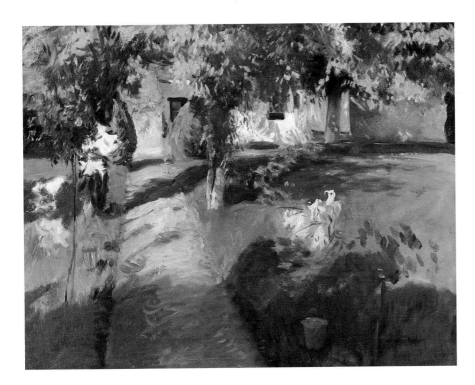

SARGENT
Millet's Garden, 1886
Oil on canvas, 27×34″
Private Collection

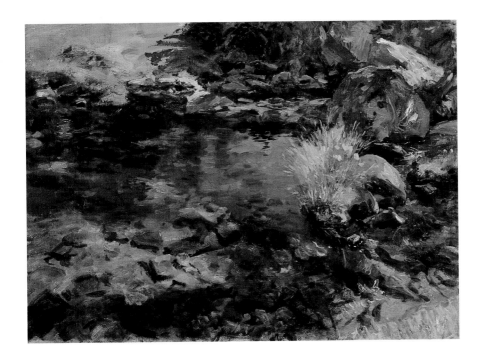

SARGENT
Alpine Pool, 1909
Oil on canvas, 27¹/₂×38″
The Metropolitan Museum of
Art, New York. Gift of
Mrs. Francis Ormond, 1950

had a heavy acidulous way of painting grass, and the paintings of his that most successfully employed the light, glinting Impressionist palette have little vegetation in them — in *Teresa Gosse,* the elfin little girl is seen against a sky so scrubby as to be abstract, and in *Near the Mount of Olives,* not much is growing on the stony ground. Water, on the other hand, was a congenial substance: the semi-transparence of shallow depths distinguishes *Alpine Pool,* and in two rapid paintings of his sister Violet (*Violet Fishing, Autumn on the River*), the monotone bars of reflection in the rippling river seem somehow Sargent's own, an effect he noticed and transcribed without Monet's example controlling him.

Where Courbet rather than Monet haunts the canvas, Sargent could paint a fine open-air picture. The very early *Oyster Gatherers of Cancale,* with its procession across blue-puddled sand beneath a cloud-patched sky, tastes vividly of salt and air, and *Capri,* of a few years later, makes music visible in the two small figures atop the white wall, a stretched-out chanter and a swinging dancer. Toward the other end of his productive life, he was improving as a watercolorist. *Villa di Marlia, Lucca,* done in

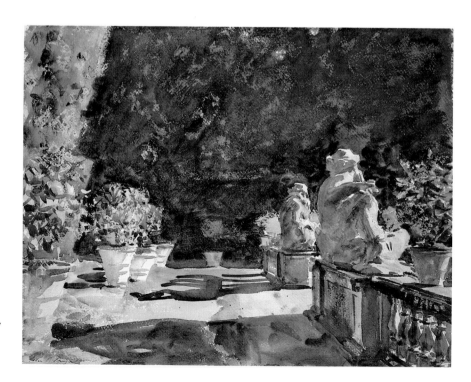

SARGENT
Villa di Marlia, Lucca, c. 1910
Watercolor on paper, 15 3/4 × 20 3/4"
Museum of Fine Arts, Boston
Charles Henry Hayden Fund

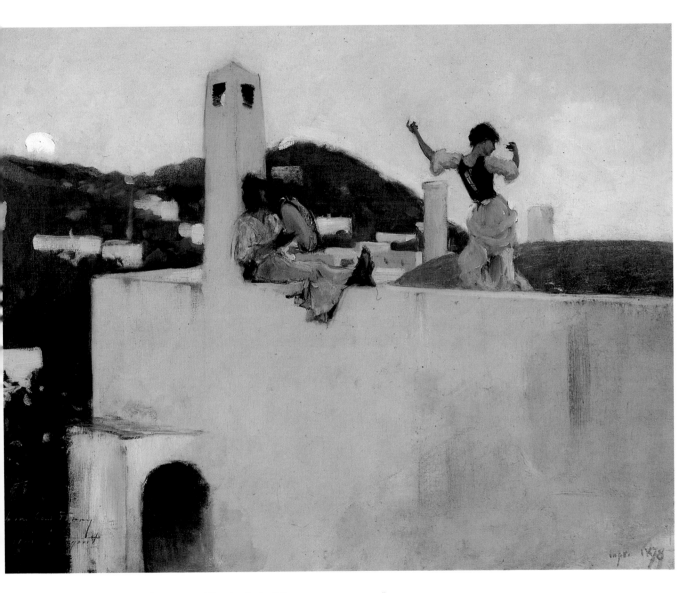

SARGENT *Capri*, 1878. Oil on canvas, 20×25″
The Warner Collection of Gulf States Paper Corporation, Tuscaloosa, Alabama

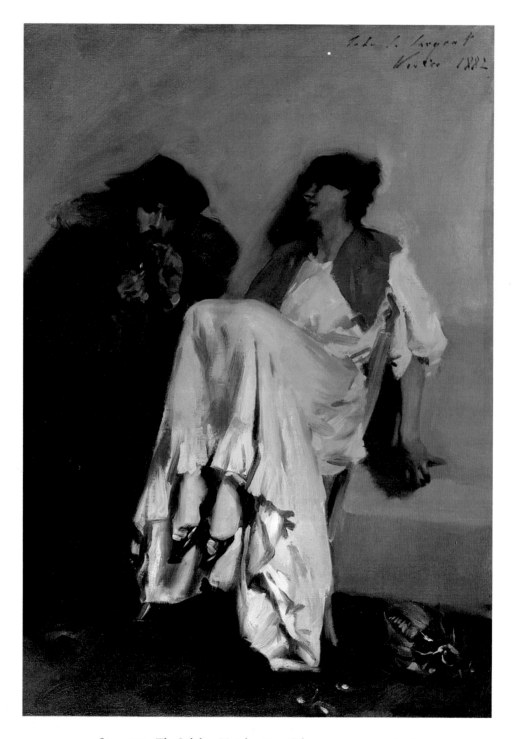

SARGENT *The Sulphur Match,* 1882. Oil on canvas, 23 × 16¹/₄″
Courtesy of Mr. and Mrs. Hugh Halff, Jr.

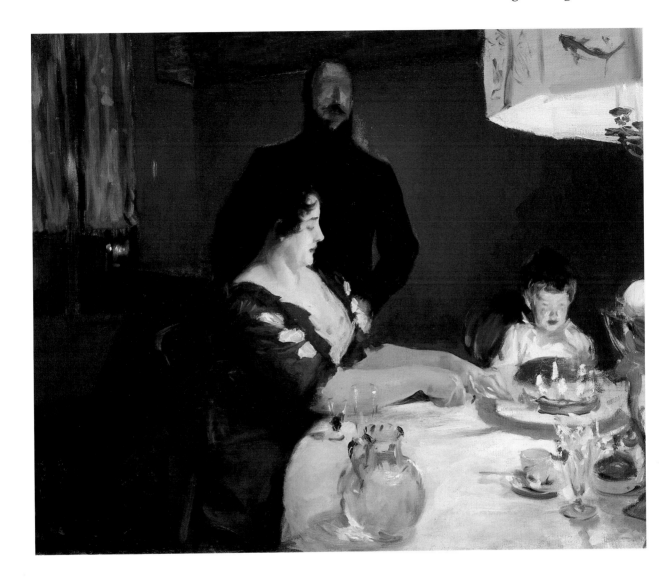

1910, has the kind of purely coloristic life absent from his oil landscapes, and that monumentality which arises—again and again, in the work of Cézanne—from sheer veracity of seeing. Of the Venice paintings, *The Sulphur Match* is a perfect little oil, swift as a sideways glance. And a charming anecdotal painting of a birthday party in the Albert Besnard family—the plump mother daintily cutting the cake whose candlelight blanches the face of the off-center child, while the father looms behind them as black as the thought of death—suggests that Sargent, had he stayed in

SARGENT
*Fête Familiale:
The Birthday Party,* 1885
Oil on canvas, 24 × 29″
The Minneapolis Institute of Arts. The Ethel Morrison and John R. Van Derlip Funds

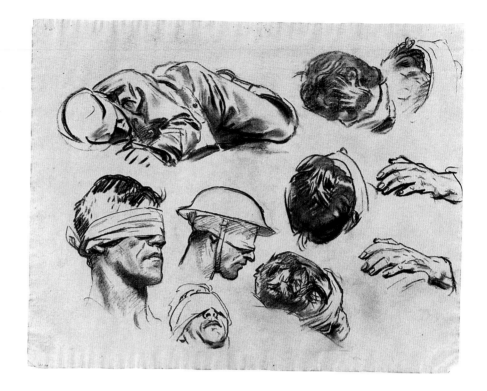

France, might have joined and enriched that stagestruck, semi-caricatural line from Daumier to Degas and Toulouse-Lautrec. A visitor to the Whitney should not omit to inspect the charcoal drawings. The Yeats portrait has been mentioned; there is also a superb drawing of Nijinsky, some unexpectedly moving studies of soldiers at the front in World War I, and a most beautifully drawn baby—Sargent, indeed, is so strong a draftsman in black and white that one wonders why he seems never to have interested himself in etching.

The very listing of scattered highlights emphasizes, however, the something scattered, the something *ungathered,* about Sargent's use of his great gifts. "He can do anything, and don't know himself what he can do," his fellow artist Edwin Austin Abbey wrote of him as late as 1890. "He is latent with all manner of possibility." One trouble might have been that Sargent imbibed enough of the French avant-garde and the art-for-art's-sake philosophy of Wilde and Whistler to distrust portrait-making as an exercise of high art. (Had he continued to evolve, of course, he might well, like Rembrandt, have lost his sitters.) His uneasiness denied his portraits the innocence of, say, Modigliani's, and his career the exuberance of Picasso's or Rubens's, to name two other tireless and fluent workers. This uneasiness, artistically sublimated into stabbing brushwork and edgy poses, may relate, of course, to his unsettled upbringing, in a family that moved back and forth across Europe from one rental to another.

His father, Dr. Fitzwilliam Sargent, was an up-and-coming medical practitioner—the author and illustrator of the standard work on bandaging, used by both sides during the Civil War—from a solid Philadelphia family. At the age of thirty-four, in deference to his grieving wife's nervous symptoms after the death of their two-year-old daughter, he took her on a trip to Europe. The excursion never ended; Mary Singer Sargent's health continued uncertain enough to keep them perpetually abroad, though she was well enough to give birth to five more children, of whom the oldest was John. John Singer Sargent took pride in being American, but he didn't see this country until he was eleven, and only in the last decade of his life did he spend much time here. Henry James's expatriation, like Whistler's, was purposeful and willed, whereas Sargent's had

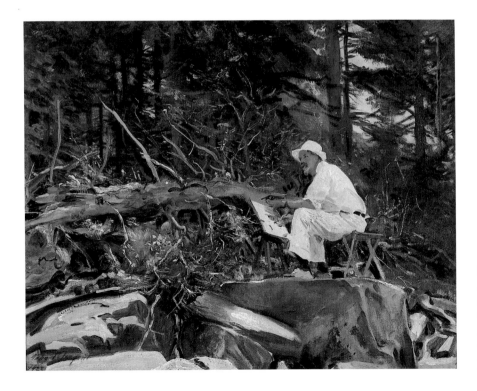

SARGENT
Portrait of the Artist Sketching, 1922
Oil on canvas, 22 × 28″
Museum of Art, Rhode Island School of Design. Gift of Mrs. Houghton Metcalf

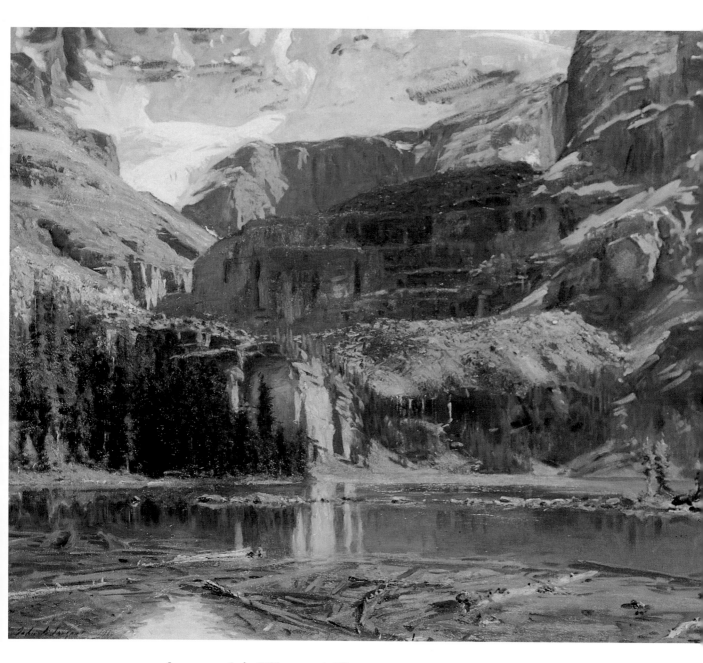

SARGENT   *Lake O'Hara*, 1916. Oil on canvas, 37 1/4 × 44"
Harvard University Art Museums, Fogg Art Museum, Cambridge, Massachusetts
Louise G. Bettens Fund

been wished upon him from birth. His nature was pliant and resourceful enough to make the best of it, and to carry his mother and surviving sisters into fame and prosperity with him. But when the visitor to the Whitney goes downstairs one flight and looks at the Hopper or two hanging in the permanent collection, he can feel what he has been missing: an undercurrent of emotion bred of the deep acquaintance that can take a landscape and its inhabitants to be a vocabulary, a set of wordless symbols effortlessly shared.

What did the English upper crust in its boots and furbelows mean to Sargent? What, even, did the straw-hatted boatmen and rosy-cheeked midinettes dear to Impressionism mean to him? He came back, with his British accent and the massive embonpoint earned at a thousand dinner parties, to the United States, and to New England, because mural commissions abounded in Boston; the two paintings of latest provenance at the Whitney exhibition testify that he also did some *plein-air* paintings here. *Portrait of the Artist Sketching* of 1922 shows his friend Dwight Blaney seated at an easel on a rock, in a pine woods: the tall, resolutely brown trees let through dabs of sunlight and one of them has fallen, creating a tangle of dead branches and splintered trunk in the near-foreground. It is recognizably an American forest, and looks better, and relates better to its solitary figure, than Sargent's color-streaked Impressionist groves. And some years earlier, the supercivilized expatriate undertook, gamely enough, a camping trip to the Rockies, and brought back a number of pictures, including this show's *Lake O'Hara*. It depicts a lake of a dead-green color that rings true in this remoteness, with stratified orange rocks above, relieved by shaggy pines, and yielding, at the top of the canvas, to snow slopes whose summits we do not see. A litter of floating logs in the foreground is brushed in roughly, in neutral color. The unrelieved North American wilderness makes a somber, simple, grandly raw landscape, innocent of human beings and of unease. Nature is impassive, and so is the art. The one thing American about Sargent was the wilderness in his eye.

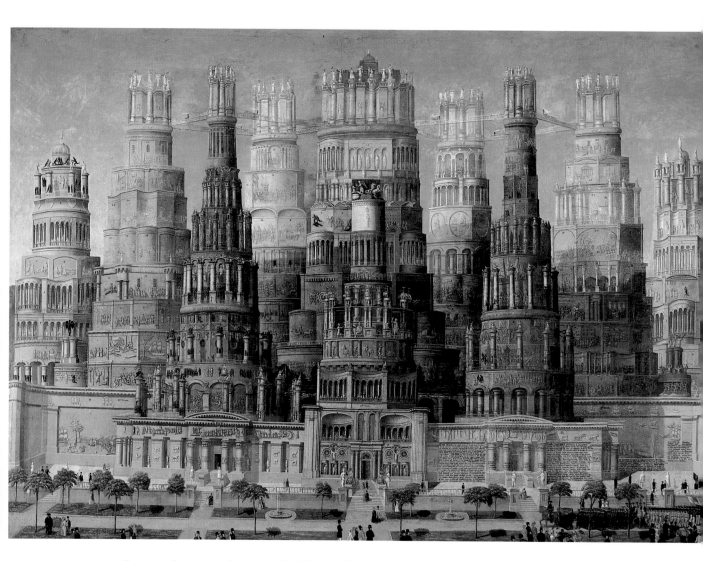

ERASTUS SALISBURY FIELD   *The Historical Monument of the American Republic,* 1867 and 1888
Oil on canvas, 9′3″ × 13′1″. Museum of Fine Arts, Springfield, Massachusetts
The Morgan Wesson Memorial Collection

Field's Luminous Folk

THE LIFE of Erastus Salisbury Field (1805–1900) encompassed almost all of the nineteenth century. His career was broken in half by the invention of photography; the market for his formal yet vital portraits of rural New Englanders dried up with the spread, in the 1840s, of the daguerreotype. Pliantly enough, he went to New York and learned the new art, and his portraits after 1850 are based upon photographic originals, which they copy, enlarge upon, and assemble into family groups. But the artist in him had flown portraiture and took perch in elaborate, studious fantasies, of Biblical scenes and of patriotic wedding cakes that would not and could not ever be built, even if, as he helpfully suggested in a pamphlet accompanying his most grandiose scheme, *The Historical Monument of the American Republic,* they be filled up "with stones or concrete in one solid mass, all but the center and the entrance through each Tower." He was trying to be practical. If the photographer's studio had made the travelling portrait-painter obsolete, there was still some popular audience for the illustrated lecture, the public mural, and the panorama; Field himself had seen in mid-century New York a five-mile panorama of a voyage around the world, beginning and ending in Boston. His later work derives from prints and book illustrations and chromolithographs showing the Taj Mahal and Egyptian temples, the armies of the pharaoh and of General Washington, of General Grant awkwardly seated upon an

FIELD
Garden of Eden, c. 1860
Oil on canvas, 25 × 41 1/2"
Shelburne Museum,
Shelburne, Vermont

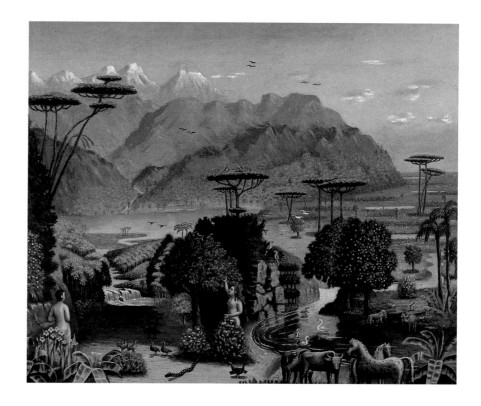

elephant and Eve awkwardly nude in the Garden of Eden. It is an art of the
not there as definitely as his portraits are an art of the *there*, of the visible
and vivid individual presence. His total œuvre, then, gives us, serially, the
outside and the inside of nineteenth-century America: the stiff-garbed,
frilled, ringleted gentlemen and gentlewomen who eye us with unflinch-
ing, just barely smiling rectitude; and the lush patriotic and religious vi-
sions that uplifted and guided them through their workdays and Sundays.

Field was an undersized, churchgoing Yankee with a receding chin; he
spent most of his life in the countrified territory of Leverett, Massachusetts, in the Connecticut Valley, and, long after his life's dust settled, he
became the subject of two separate Manhattan shows in the fall of 1984.
One of these showed at the Museum of American Folk Art but, though
his draftsmanship has something primitive about it, Field was scarcely
a folk artist; he studied under Samuel F. B. Morse, a distinguished academic painter before he became an inventor, and Field supplied a professional product to satisfied customers. Like all customers of a real

artist, his got a little more than they bargained for. Though his representations have as much anatomy as the figures on playing cards, their faces display a vital tension and luminousness, and a complex inner life. Is Louisa Cowls, in her lovely lace collar, disapproving of us, or flirting with us? Is there a pinch of weakness in the corner of Amos Hulbert's mouth, and a wateriness to his eyes? These heads resemble those on Gothic cathedral portals in their transcendent individuality, their encapsulation, each, of an eternally valued soul. Their spirituality is visually emphasized by a stylized gray billowing behind them, or smears of mysterious light. Where Field chooses to give us a glimpse of the earth that upholds his gazing Christians, he can achieve a sumptuous, Italianate effect, as in the miniature brick city that picks up the red of Louisa Gallond Cook's lips, her ruby brooch, her knuckles, and the drape behind her. Field's females, in an age and place that relegated sensuality to the barn and backwoods, arrest and command the viewer; his sister-in-law, bearing the Bunyan-esque name of Thankful Field Field (Field's wife was called Phebe, and his twin sister Salome), is coolly, solidly beautiful, with an erotically exposed

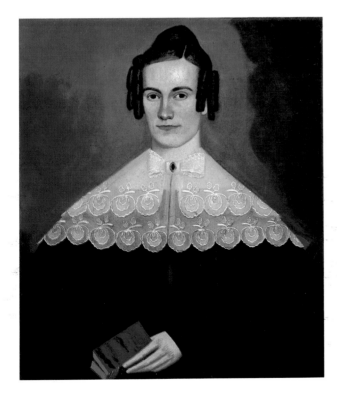

FIELD
Louisa Cowls, 1837
Oil on canvas, 30¹/₄ × 26¹/₈"
Worcester Art Museum,
Worcester, Massachusetts

FIELD
Thankful Field Field, c. 1835
Oil on canvas, 31 1/4 × 25 5/8″
Museum of Fine Arts,
Springfield, Massachusetts
The Morgan Wesson Memorial
Collection

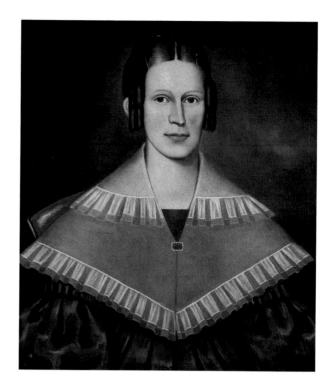

throat. Her beauty would feel like smooth wood to the touch; the beauty
of Mrs. Charles Ball Nye is softer, hazier, more questing—a vulnerable
femininity doubled by that of her infant daughter. And Mary Valonia
Robbins looks downright sulky and spoiled; we can imagine this face
with a punk haircut.

Many of the faces seem modern because they are accurately observed,
and, unlike costumes and prevailing convictions, faces are subject to no
historical mode, just an endless genetic recycling. Field's differ from
daguerreotypes in that the details have been processed by a mind and
hand; Mr. Pearce's brass buttons, ribbed shirtfront, red-headed sunburn,
and pale high forehead were assembled consciously, and in sum constitute
a social opinion, an impression one man has made upon another. When
Field, as a painter, turned to his imagination, the luminosity of his faces
gave way to a gloomy, lurid palette; in his Eden or Egypt we feel locked
into a terrible Victorian indoors, surrounded by musty scrapbooks. His
painted landscape of Rattlesnake Gutter—splashes of water and gowned

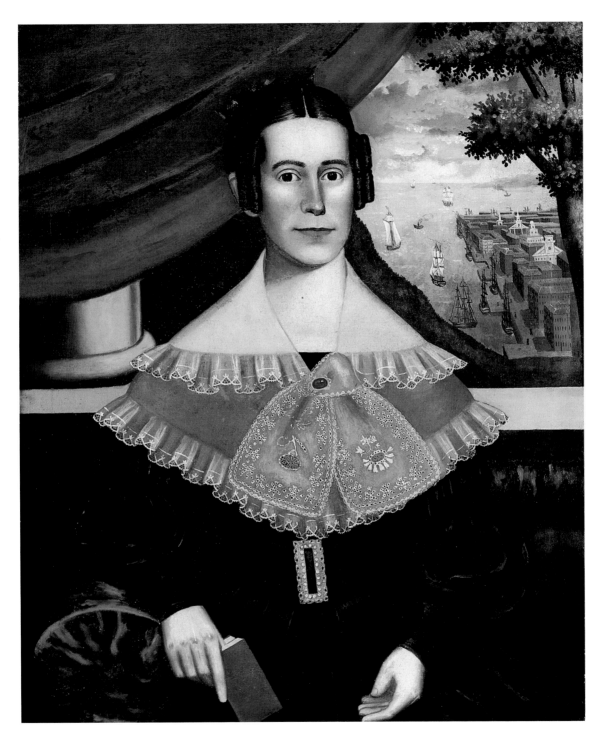

FIELD   *Louisa Ellen Gallond Cook*, c. 1839. Oil on canvas, 34×28″
Shelburne Museum, Shelburne, Vermont

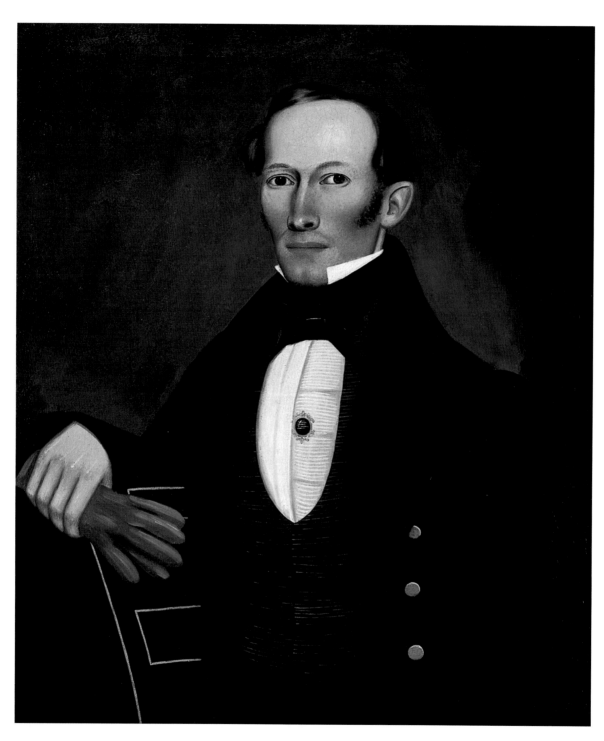

FIELD   *Mr. Pearce*, c. 1838. Oil on canvas, 30 × 26″
The Abby Aldrich Rockefeller Folk Art Center, Williamsburg, Virginia

sightseers almost lost in the dark of the American forest—shows this same gloom, the gorgy gloom of the uncleared land, and we realize why Field's portraits have a contrasting ebullience and candlelit warmth. Stiffly holding their fans and flutes and books and quills, his citizens bask in the glow of civilization, in having wrested, from the surly, tangled continent, a certain comfort and order.

FIELD
Rattlesnake Gutter, c. 1855
Oil on canvas, 30½″ × 27½″
Private collection

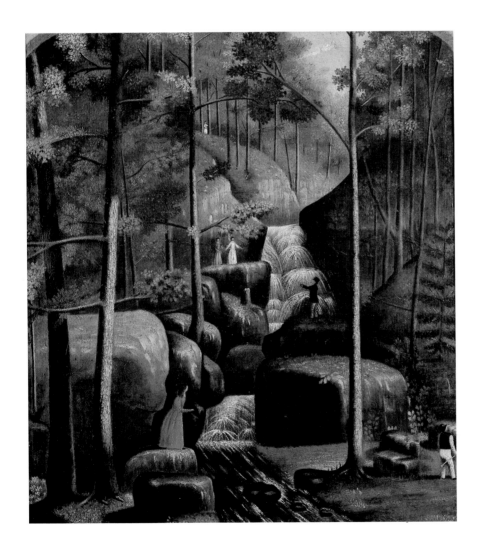

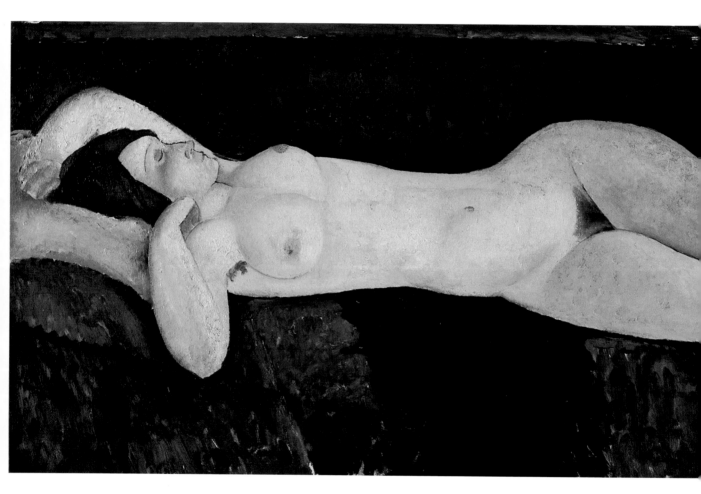

AMEDEO MODIGLIANI   *Reclining Nude,* c. 1919. Oil on canvas, 28 1/2 × 45 7/8″
The Museum of Modern Art, New York. Mrs. Simon Guggenheim Fund

A Case of Solicitude

Reclining Nude, or *Le Grand Nu,* is the largest of the series of nudes Amedeo Modigliani painted between 1916 and 1919; it hangs in the expanded Museum of Modern Art, next to the exit from a heavily trafficked room, in a position so exposed and vulnerable that I once wrote a letter to the director of the museum about it, expressing my anxiety that someone, in a world where hatred of beautiful things always lurks, would take the moment needed to slash this gorgeous canvas with a knife or scribble over it with a Magic Marker. The director, an old college classmate of mine, ignored my letter, and the painting remains next to the doorway, and has not yet been harmed. Modigliani's paintings, having already survived the wreck of their creator's violent, alcohol-soaked life, are perhaps tougher than I solicitously imagine.

But few nudes, not even Giorgione's *Sleeping Venus* or Goya's *Maja Desnuda,* expose their tender white fronts to us so trustingly, or so dramatically illustrate Karl Barth's dictum that woman "is in her whole existence an appeal to the kindness of man." This woman is paler than most of her sisters in Modigliani's œuvre, where skin tends to be ruddy or golden. Her pallor flows like a river between the dark banks of the vaguely indicated coverings of her couch. Her elongated torso links two bulging masses, one of them her hips and the other a complicated close lumping of arms, breasts, and head; this long middle softly twists, for the triangle of pubic hair confronts us frontally, while her breasts are shown in three-quarter view, and her face in profile. Her profile is drawn upon her flesh with a fastidious black line, of which her eyebrow is a detached, floating arc. We savor and cherish the patches of pink that she holds in her hands (curled in sleep like those of a baby), and that tinge with a flush her cheeks and eyelid, and that mark her nipples. Without these rosy touches, her form might be too absolute.

How odd that Modigliani, whose life was such a turbulent and defiant squandering, drew and painted with such serene limpidity, and of modern artists adhered most closely to the classic and Renaissance ideal of design extracted from an attentive rendition of the real. Here, the dark red above and the various saturnine colors below press upon the model with exquisite, simplified curves that clarify without suppressing the call of her flesh. The composition is blunt and the foreground was scrubbed in with a visible impatience, and yet life and air are present, distilled into a sweet and triumphant sensation. Women *do* feel to us this long and gently undulant

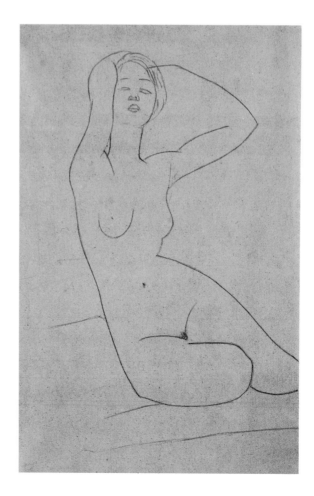

MODIGLIANI
Seated Nude, c. 1918
Pencil, 17³/8 × 11″
The Museum of Modern Art,
New York. Gift of Abby Aldrich
Rockefeller

in the waist, and *are* this grand in self-forgetfulness. How odd, too, that, for all Modigliani's facility and haste and the something mannered and formulaic in his mature style, so little of his work seems automatic, or sinks into kitsch. His nudes (unlike those of Renoir) are individual women, with various live expressions on their faces; it may have been this psychological realism, as much as the pubic hair the painter insisted on indicating, that caused the police to remove five nude paintings from Modigliani's only one-man show during his lifetime, at the Berthe Weil Gallery in 1917.

He was the most spectacular of the so-called *peintres maudits*—the accursed painters—who flocked to the bohemia of Paris early in the century. It took a heavy curse, of bad luck and bad self-management, to deny an artist of such accessible and conservative gifts the popularity that descended as soon as he was dead, in 1920. He was the coddled, sickly son of Sephardic Jews settled in Livorno; he was well educated and well acquainted with the art treasures of Italy. He painted only from life, drank while he painted, and liked to complete a canvas in one sitting. The poet Max Jacob said of his friend: "Everything in him tended toward purity in art. His unsupportable pride, his black ingratitude, his haughtiness . . . Yet all that was nothing but a need for crystalline purity, a trueness to himself in life as in art. He was cutting, but as fragile as glass; also as inhuman as glass, so to say." The purity and fragility are here in *Le Grand Nu,* in the defenseless globular whiteness of her breasts, in the fleshly softness that gives her abdomen a perceptible droop. Yet also the cuttingness—a generalizing power that bestows upon this nude the archaic simplicity Modigliani had sought in sculpture, which had been his first love. She is Woman in her primeval aspect, stylized and exaggerated with the ruthlessness of African sculpture, though colored as sensuously as a Titian. If we look at her sideways, as if she were standing, we see how anatomically impossible she is—how expressionistically, that is, the painter has rendered her horizontal relaxation into sleep. She seems her own dream, and we fear to have her sleep disturbed.

The last time I was in the Museum of Modern Art, I observed that a pane of glareless glass had been inserted in the frame of *Reclining Nude,* protecting her from Magic Markers and X-acto knives. Had it been there all along? Or had my solicitude elicited this measure from my old classmate? If the latter is true, I feel I have entered, in a minute way, art history—have reached out toward a masterpiece, and touched it.

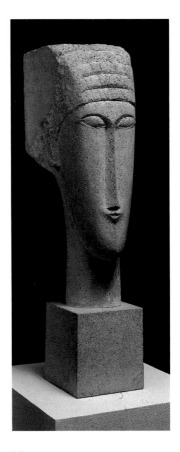

MODIGLIANI
Head (Tête), 1911–1913
Limestone
25 × 6 × 8 1/2″
The Solomon R. Guggenheim
Museum, New York

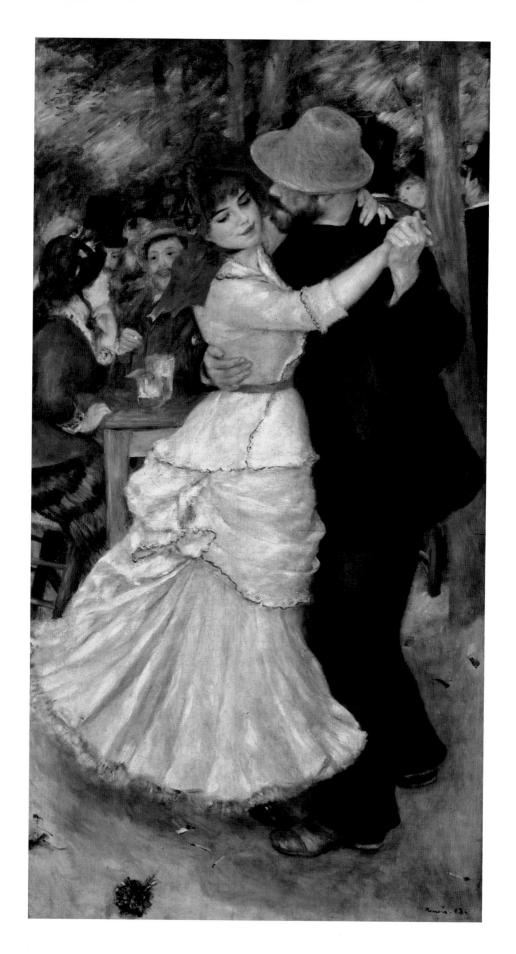

Is Art Worth It?

BOSTON's publicity drums have been throbbing for months in anticipation of 1985's Renoir show at the Museum of Fine Arts. An article in the August 20th Boston *Globe* portrayed William Murphy, "director of operations," standing "hunched over a blueprint with red and green lines marking viewing paths and guard stations snaking through the galleries." "Publicity officer" Christopher Bowden was quoted as crowing, "There'll be pictures, Renoir posters, Renoir books. Renoir T-shirts and sweat shirts. Renoir buttons." Thirty-six thousand five-dollar tickets had already been sold as of the first week of August; half a million people were expected; staff members were close to buckling under the immense pressure from friends and relatives for Renoir-oriented favors; shuttle buses from Copley Square and crowd-counting photoelectric cells were in the works. The invasion of Grenada hadn't warranted more logistics than this "megashow." Museum "officials," with a nostalgic backward glance to the "New World" exhibit of two years ago, when the weight of the crowds more than once broke the escalators, reassured the obviously alarmed reporter that "High-interest shows such as Renoir are necessary . . . to boost attendance and broaden the museum's base."

My wife and I, as museum members, received frequent bulletins as to the show's grandeur and the prodigious difficulties bound to assail those who attempted to see it. Important-looking polychrome tickets by Tick-

PIERRE-AUGUSTE RENOIR
Dance at Bougival, 1882–83
Oil on canvas, 71 1/2 × 38 1/2"
Museum of Fine Arts, Boston
Picture Fund

etron arrived in the mail, assigning us a precise admission time on one of the members' days, before the universal onrush. We were warned that the parking around the museum and in its newish, I. M. Pei–designed parking lot would be impossible, and so it proved. Traffic on Huntington Avenue slowed to a honking, snarling crawl as we neared the citadel of art. Panicked lest we miss our appointed hour and be relegated to a dark afternoon in remotest December, we found an illegal spot in some mazy casbah off the Fenway and scurried pell-mell through the thickening mobs. Inside the formerly stately museum, hullabaloo had attained a carnival pitch; the crush at the cloakroom merged indistinguishably with the crush at the admission counter. Upstairs, at the head of the not-as-yet-broken escalator, two infinite parallel lines had formed: one for the 12:30 people, and one for the one o'clocks, which included us. Things were running, rumor had it, forty-five minutes late. My mind fled back to the *Globe* article, and Director of Operations Murphy's guarded estimate: "We'll set an arbitrary level of 700 people at a time. As long as the average stay isn't over an hour, we're OK." Evidently, the individual viewing time for the ninety-seven assembled paintings was exceeding the projected thirty-seven seconds each.

Our line, though long and unmoving, was good-tempered. We were, after all, museum members—tiny art patrons. Half of the males looked like George Bush at assorted points in his evolution, wearing end-of-summer suits and that blinking, stooping air of wry martyrdom with which Boston-area men escort their wives to cultural events; and the other half looked like post-*Howl* Allen Ginsberg, outfitted by L. L. Bean. There seemed to be, perhaps in response to Renoir's love of young flesh, a remarkable number of babies, harnessed to their parents by a well-stitched wealth of slings, knapsacks, and neo-papooses. Rain beat gently on the skylights as we shuffled our way, with nary a sideways glance, through the dim chambers of Tibetan art, where three-eyed godlings danced in eternal fire. Less than an hour behind schedule, we were admitted to the fulgent galleries where the show hung. It is no small compliment to Renoir's vitality to say that he wasn't trampled underfoot.

The paintings made their splashes, in their ornate old plaster frames, on the blue-gray wall, and some were indeed splendid. But such a concentration, after such hoopla, made it clearer than it should have been that Renoir does not quite rank with the heroic masters of early modern painting—specifically, with his friends Monet and Cézanne. Compared

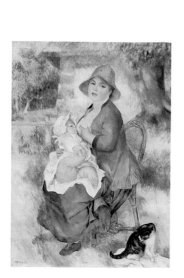

RENOIR
The Child at the Breast
(or *Maternity*), 1886
Oil on canvas, 29 × 21″
Private collection of Mr. and
Mrs. Hermann Schnabel

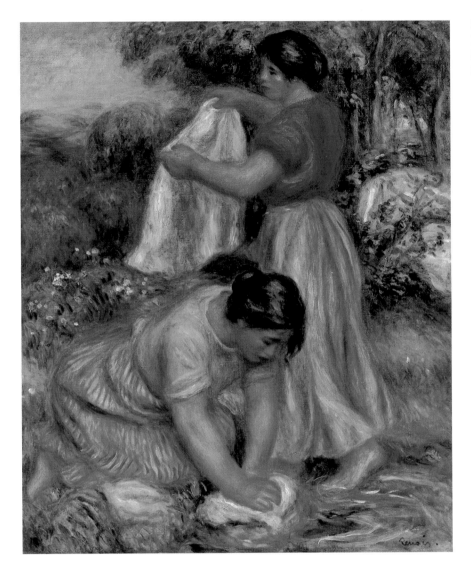

RENOIR
Two Washerwomen, c. 1912
Oil on canvas, 25³/₄ × 21¹/₂″
Private collection

with either, he didn't look hard enough. He saw what he wanted to see, and turned it as he aged into an inward vision, a mythology. The shimmering, breezy outdoors of Impressionism gradually grows furry and comes indoors and in the end becomes a kind of tapestry, a green-and-blue background scrubbed in behind nudes painted in quite another style, a style of enamelled pallor. The brushstrokes turn greasier, the colors rawer, the drawing vaguer. In the end the people all look Mexican, and a lumpy muralism reminds us that Renoir began to paint as a decorator of porcelain, fans, blinds, and walls. Old artists are entitled to caricature themselves, but—though his huge pottery women are said to have inspired Picasso in one of his phases—Renoir's final turn is less usefully, less searchingly extreme than Monet's virtually abstract water lilies or Cézanne's sketchy, segmented watercolors, which showed the way to Cubism.

Such is the sour mood of unappreciation induced by a megashow. Poor Renoir, he didn't ask for this. Placed in the Impressionist/ Post-Impressionist galleries of a major museum, a half-dozen canvases by him speak with their own charming accent and glow by their own tender light. But the numerous paintings in Boston, dutifully consumed by the eyeball as one shuffles past in a slow pedestrian choo-choo, begin to deposit on the retina an accumulated taste of artificial sweetener. Somewhere between the spanking fresh outdoor studies of the 1870s and the baby-pale nudes of the next decade, Renoir's coloring becomes artificial—his greens harder and bluer than vegetation, his skin tones devoid of real shadow, a sickly ochre haunting his outdoors and indoors. The faces of his females develop their characteristic look, of coal-dark eyes burning in milk-white faces. The little *Gypsy Girl* of 1879 is one of the last portraits that provides the sensation of an individual presence—her frizzy body of reddish hair, the curiously tentative, agape expression of her mouth. And her figure and clothes are one with the outdoor background, within a palpable atmosphere. In the two spectacular *Blonde Bathers* of 1881 and 1882, atmosphere has been sacrificed to a sensual monumentality, and the blue-soaked background is mostly backdrop—gold-tinged crags and cardboard sea fetched from a book of fairy tales to set off our plump mermaids. Aline Charigot, the dressmaker who eventually became Madame Renoir, said that she was still very thin when, at the age of twenty-two, on a trip to Italy, she struck this pose for her lover: Renoir's homage put the fat into infatuation, and also placed a wedding ring on her left hand, nine years before they actually married. The first *Blonde Bather* was painted from life, and the second from the first; the edges have become sharper and less plausible, the blue of the sea and the red of her hair have unreally intensified, and her dazzlingly pale

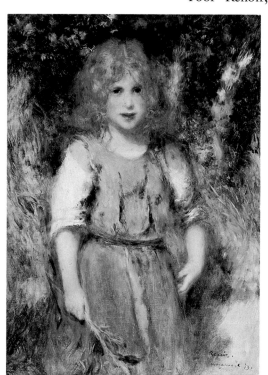

RENOIR
Gypsy Girl, 1879
Oil on canvas, 28 1/2 × 21"
Private collection, Canada

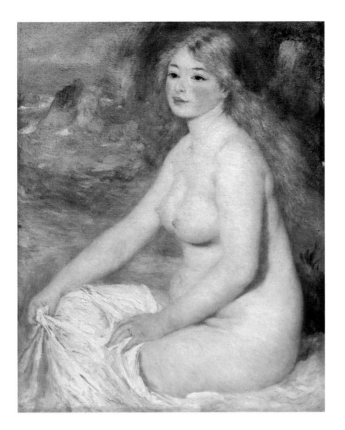

RENOIR
Blonde Bather I, 1881–82
Oil on canvas, 32 × 26″
Sterling and Francine Clark Art
Institute, Williamstown,
Massachusetts

flesh, which in the first version carried some modelling shadows of complementary color, in the second is baldly shadowed with pink. We are on the verge here of poster art.

Onions and the blossoming trees of *The Seine at Chatou,* both from 1881, show that Renoir could still paint what was before him, in his feathery, flicking strokes. The kind of purely visual excitement, however, that could turn a bit of Algerian landscape (1881) into a florid storm of tans and browns and flecks of black, soon yields to the postcard tints of *Landscape near Menton* (1883), the stately anecdotes of the three tall dancing couples of 1882–83, and his labored attempts, in the quest for an art that would give back classic dignity to the human figure, to imitate the drier, paler, more composed look of quattrocento frescoes. His great mock-fresco is the large *Bathers* (1887), to be found in the Philadelphia Museum of Art; Boston displays from this period the very stiff and (except for the lefthand child) dull portrait of the Berard children at Wargemont,

RENOIR
(Right) *Onions*, 1881
Oil on canvas, 15 1/2 × 23 1/2″
Sterling and Francine Clark Art
Institute, Williamstown,
Massachusetts

(Below) *Algerian Landscape:
The Ravin de la Femme
Sauvage*, 1881
Oil on canvas, 25 1/2 × 32″
Musée d'Orsay, Paris

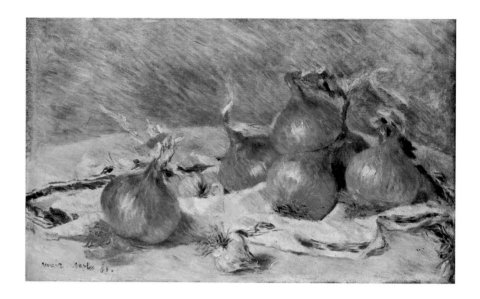

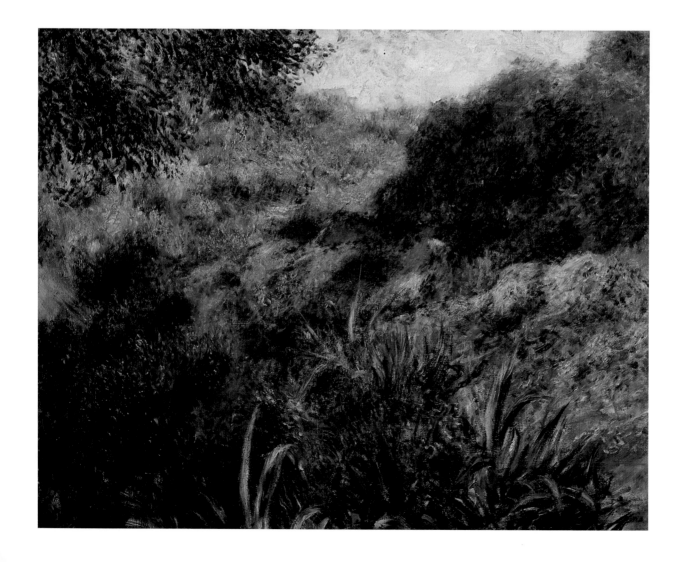

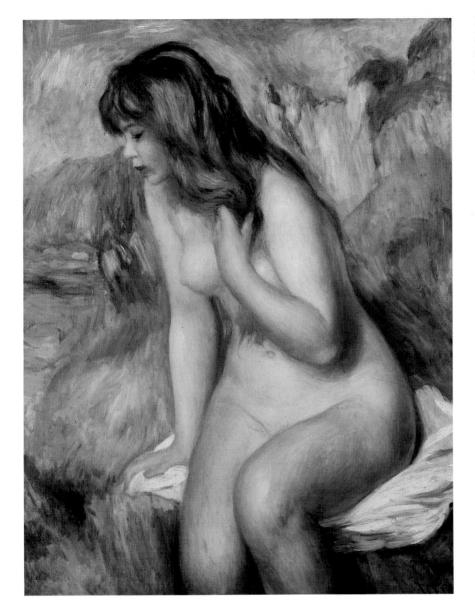

RENOIR
Bather, 1892
Oil on canvas, 31 1/2 × 25″
Archives Durand-Ruel, Paris

one of the many amiable society portraits the painter executed. Renoir was, like Velázquez and Sargent, a student of children, of their little plump, blurred, half-asleep faces. The two nude *Bather*s of 1892 and 1895 rather shockingly have, atop their lush womanly bodies, the heads of little girls; the *Blonde Bather*s from the early Eighties, in their idealized

RENOIR
*Portrait of Mademoiselle
Romaine Lacaux,* 1864
Oil on canvas, 32 × 25 ¹/₂″
The Cleveland Museum of Art
Gift of the Hanna Fund

pink-white roundnesses, impose regression on the entire body: Venus as baby. The peaceable Renoir moment is a kind of naptime; his dancing couples drowse in one another's arms, and his outdoor cafés exist without clatter or the possibility of conflict. He repeatedly insisted that he painted for pleasure alone: "For me a picture . . . should be something likable, joyous and pretty—yes, pretty. There are enough ugly things in life for us not to add to them."

From his art we might imagine him a plump, rosy, placid man, but in fact he was bony-faced, nervous, reactionary, and restless. He changed residences often and kept experimenting with the styles of other painters. Having helped liberate painting into the open air, he itched to put it back in the museum, and pondered Ingres and painted Judgments of Paris. The most beautiful products of his last decade are the sculptures, fashioned by other hands but infused with his spirit, his search for a new classicism. The finest is *Venus Victorious;* she holds the apple Paris has awarded her: Eve redeemed. Among his peers Renoir was the great image-maker; only Van Gogh, a decade younger, is his equal in this respect. The childlike, supernatural bathers; the stunning blacks and whites of *The Loge* (present in the catalogue but confined to the Courtauld Institute in London); the gracile young women with their heads bent together over piano lessons; Aline nursing; the couple of *Dance at Bougival,* he with his red beard and yellow hat and she with her red bonnet and averted glance (used as the show's motif, on brochures, buttons, shopping bags): these images take hold of the mind, and make Renoir the people's Impressionist, and a natural for a megashow. But image-making, though it plays upon our deep instincts and desires, is not quite the same as painting, and one traverses the show's ninety-seven canvases feeling too rarely enchanted by feats of technique and structure like:

Portrait of Mademoiselle Romaine Lacaux (1864)—prim, opalescent, *pale*-eyed; apprentice work of a high order;

Flowers in a Vase (c. 1869)—if there was a flower Renoir was born to paint, it was the chrysanthemum;

The Promenade (1870)—painted heavily, yet alive with light and forest atmospherics;

The Seine at Argenteuil (1874)—like Monet, all eye and no false pleasantry;

Nude in the Sunlight (1875)—no clay goddess, a real faun-nymph, almost sinister in the dapple;

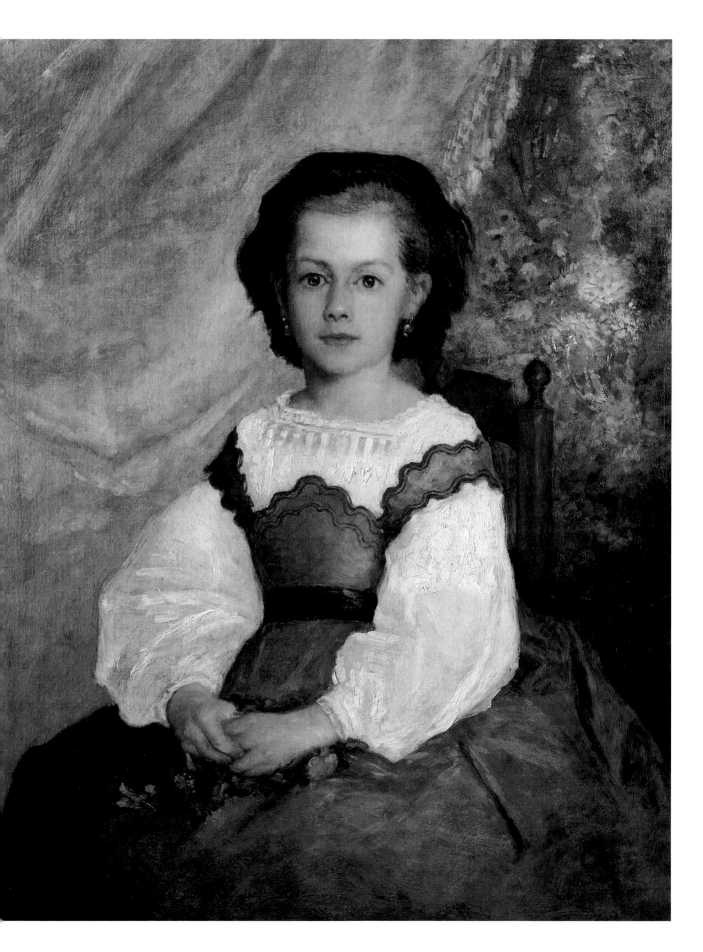

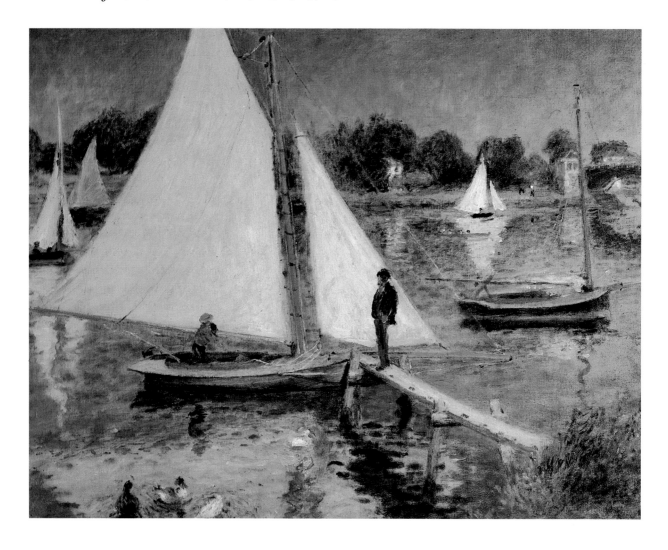

RENOIR
The Seine at Argenteuil, 1874
Oil on canvas, 20 × 25 1/2″
Portland Art Museum, Oregon
Bequest of Winslow B. Ayer

The Swing (1876)—on the edge of healthy Bonnard-like violence; the blue bows on the dress seem negatives of the dapples of sunlight all around; one of the few paintings that could be called witty; another is

Young Woman Reading an Illustrated Journal (1880–81)—not only is reading and painting an open magazine over the model's shoulder a witty thing to do, but the composition forms a sandwich of monochromes that hover like Rothko's;

Landscape at Wargemont (1879)—wonderfully weird, a winding road as a big pink worm; landscape on the verge of abstraction;

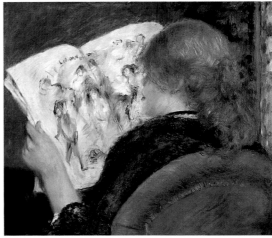

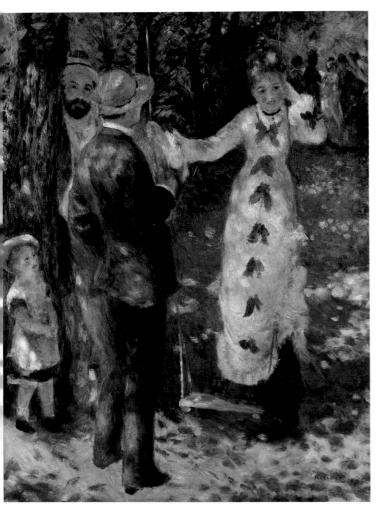

RENOIR
(Left) *The Swing (La Balançoire)*, 1876
Oil on canvas, 36 × 28 ½". Musée d'Orsay, Paris

(Above) *Young Woman Reading an Illustrated
Journal*, 1880–81. Oil on canvas, 18 ¼ × 22"
Museum of Art, Rhode Island School of Design

Sleeping Girl (1880)—that cat! that slipped strap and exposed white shoulder! an anecdotal painting we can forgive;

Dance at Bougival (1882–83)—of course; in the Boston museum's own collection, like a number of the best; I especially admired, on this viewing, the cigarette butts and matches in the foreground;

The Child at the Breast (1886)—chalky, but gives us a detailed underside of a male baby, if we care; and

Portrait of Madame Renoir with Bob (c. 1910)—presents once more his buxom Aline, the former dressmaker and artist's model, now grown gray

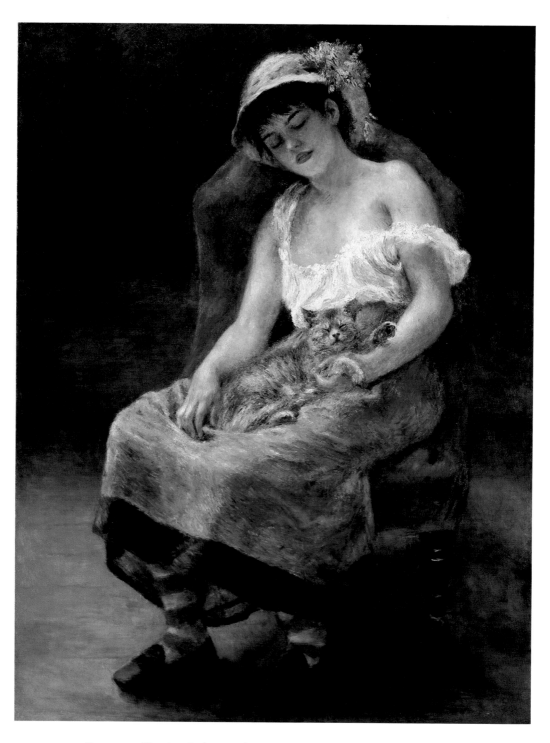

RENOIR   *Sleeping Girl* (or *Girl with a Cat*), 1880. Oil on canvas, 47 × 37″
Sterling and Francine Clark Art Institute, Williamstown, Massachusetts

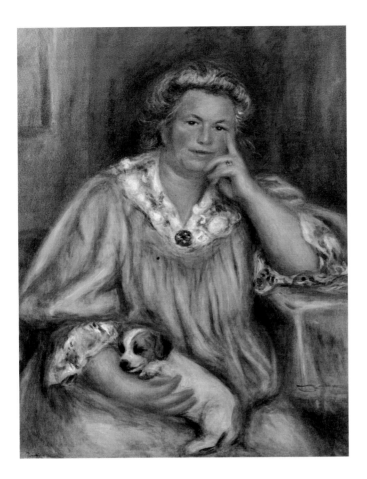

RENOIR
*Portrait of Madame Renoir
with Bob,* c. 1910
Oil on canvas, 32 × 25 ¹/₂″
Wadsworth Atheneum,
Hartford. Ella Gallup Sumner
and Mary Catlin Sumner
Collection Fund

and shrewd, with a most winningly boneless puppy in her shapeless
yellow lap.

The line at the souvenir shop was the worst yet, and the woman behind
me began to whimper that she was going to faint. Yet, with the grim forti-
tude that made New England rocky, we hung in there with our postcards
and Renoir notepaper and $19.95 catalogues, and purchased. I didn't see
anybody buying any of the fifty-cent buttons, though. As my wife and I
approached the spot where we had left our car, I espied on its windshield
a lyrical dab of color Renoir never used—Day-Glo orange, the color of a
Boston parking ticket.

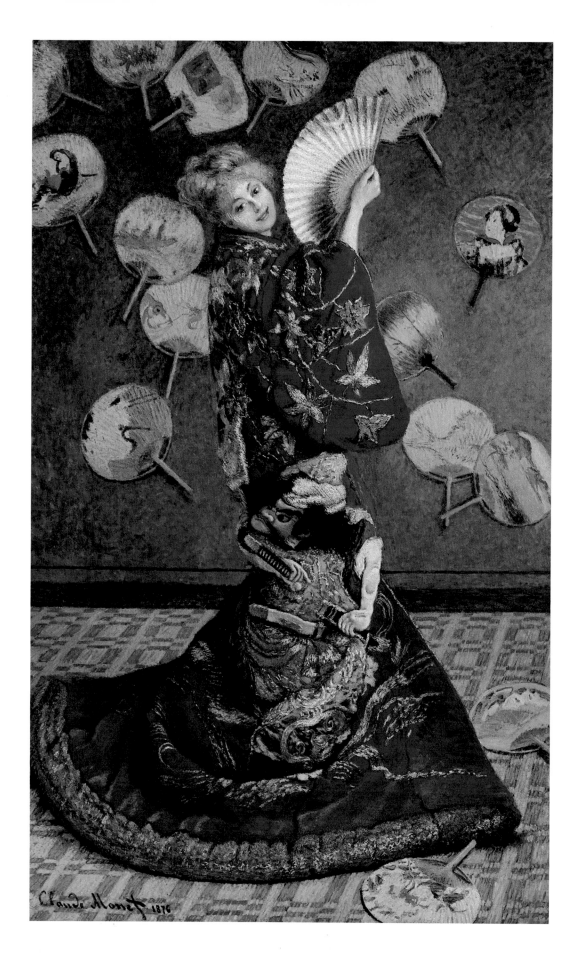

A Mischievous Monet

FOR YEARS at the Boston Museum of Fine Arts, *La Japonaise* dominated the large room of Impressionists and Post-Impressionists in which it hung. Its startling visual double-take and its exceedingly vivid red were unlike anything else in the room, where subtly tinted views of French beaches and French gardens, French still lifes and French visages formed a collective sacred hush in which this large and mischievous canvas seemed to shout out loud. The smiling woman with a grimacing samurai on her bottom even appeared unlike anything else by Monet—posed and theatrical when his usual figure studies are undramatic and casual-appearing, and devoid of the stabbing brushwork and luminous atmospherics with which, in the decade prior to this painting of 1876, he had perfected Impressionism. Monet, who imitated almost no one but Nature herself, here seems to have taken his model's head from Renoir, the studio-lit staginess from Manet, and an arch *japonaiserie* from Whistler. In 1918, when informed of this admired work's pricy resale, Monet called it *"une saleté"*—"an obscenity"—and went on to claim that it had been whipped up deliberately to make a sensation at the second Impressionist Exhibition: "They tempted me by showing me a marvelous robe on which certain gold embroideries were several centimeters thick." And it is true, a window-dressing gaudiness about the costumed woman and her ambiguous environment do give *La Japonaise,* almost uniquely in Monet's pas-

CLAUDE MONET
La Japonaise (Camille Monet in Japanese Costume), 1876
Oil on canvas, 91 1/4 × 56″
Museum of Fine Arts, Boston
1951 Purchase Fund

sionately honest œuvre, a tinge of the meretricious. The model, Monet also confided, was his wife, Camille, whom he had tricked out in a blond wig. All his denigrations delivered, however, the artist is reported to have exclaimed self-admiringly, "Look at those fabrics!"

The robe is stunningly painted. Seen full-size, the embroidered samurai, though somewhat foreshortened, seems as real as the female head above, which was rendered with a sentimental wispiness uncharacteristic of Monet. This flirtatious, slightly glazed face floats with sweet obliviousness above the turmoil of her garment, a turmoil echoed by the explosive wealth of fans suspended behind her and scattered at her feet. The sense of two creatures twisted together, amid the folds of thick cloth, affords the viewer intimations both sexual and demonic. The woman appears to be a trap in which the samurai is caught, or else a lure, with him poised to kill the prey who ventures near. The two white arms are levers of the same size, cocked one above the other in this muffled mechanism, whose murderous dynamics are diagrammed by the three arcs of her fan's edge, her sleeve's hanging edge, and the curved fold out of which his amorphous lower body rises like a dark whirlwind.

Where is she, under all this? Her body, if we believe in it, is as elongated as a stone saint's—one of those vivacious, slender figures at Moissac with

Monet
Water Lilies, c. 1920
Oil on canvas, 6′6¹⁄₂″ × 19′7¹⁄₂″
The Museum of Modern Art,
New York. Mrs. Simon
Guggenheim Fund

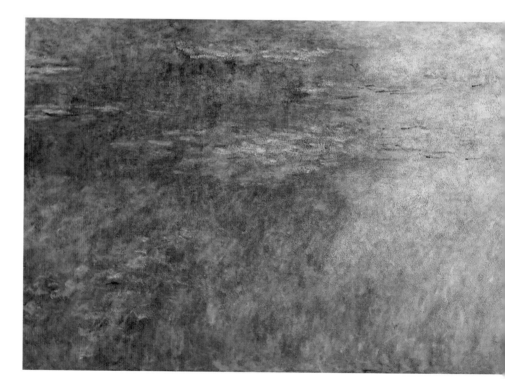

crossed legs. Possession, at the opposite pole from sainthood, might explain why her hips and legs belong not to her but to this glowering blue alien. Realistically, anthropologically, what we see here is not possession but imposition; as ancient as mankind is the impulse to paint, dust, tattoo, and scarify images upon the human skin, to improve the perishable, vulnerable body with signs and images lifted from an ideal world. So, too, the clothes and accoutrements of modern man conceal and elaborate his naked form, wrap it in stylish messages that pierce the ears, falsify the shoulders, and pinch the toes. Monet came toward the end of a century especially laden with decorative falsifications—bustles, revival architecture, figurines doubling as gas lamps, claw-footed furniture, stovepipe hats. He and his fellow Impressionists took the whole heavy Victorian brocade outdoors and gave it a shake, painting Nature in her nudity, in her radiant confusion of reflection, tint, and atmosphere. The trompe l'œil of *La Japonaise* is not so surprising, after all, from the artist whose last and mightiest project was a series of large studies of a small pond where water lilies, their trailing roots, subaqueous grass, and cloud reflections mingle on an invisible surface. Appearances deceive and enchant; Monet's work continuously celebrates the innocence of vision.

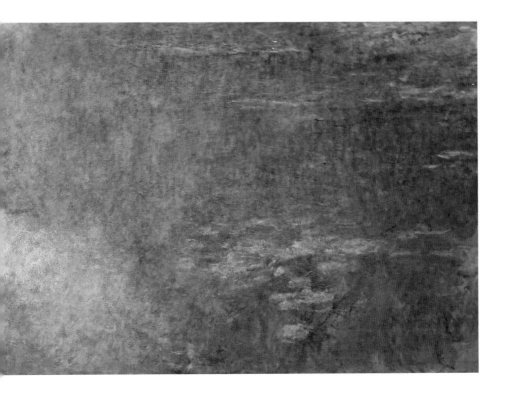

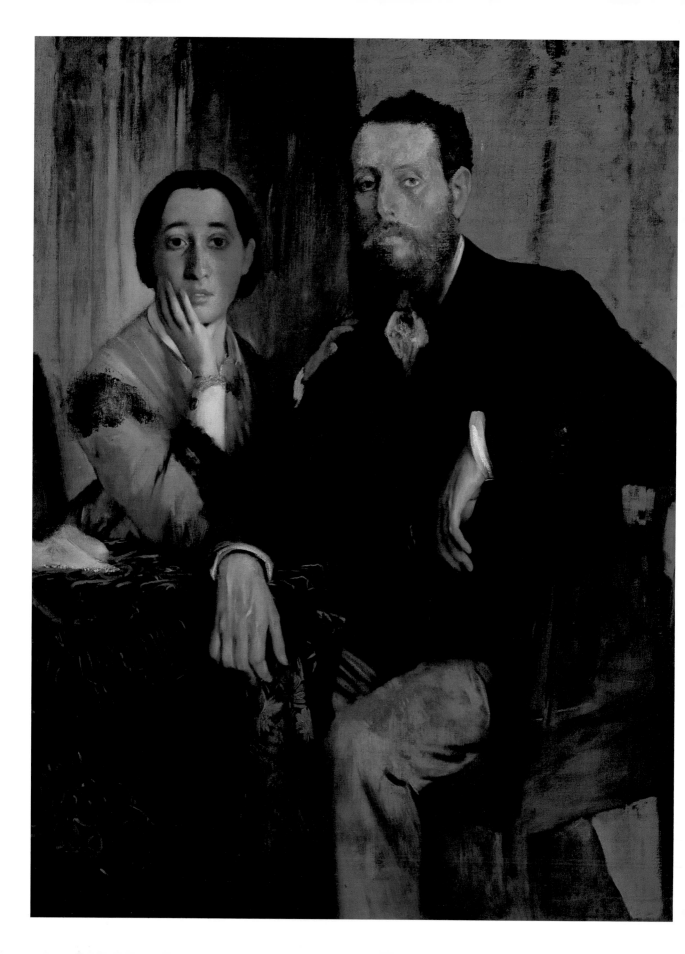

Reluctant Butterfly

———

OF THE GREAT Impressionists, Degas had the worst eyes. His myopia was
severe enough to excuse him from infantry duty; by his forties he was
virtually blind in his right eye; and by the 1890s he periodically donned
corrective spectacles blacked-out except for a small slit in the left lens.
Complaints about *la vue* recur in his letters, and late in life he wrote to a
friend, "I'll soon be a blind man. Where there are no fish, one should not
pretend to be a fisherman." He was also, of this epochal group, the most
color-shy, the least outdoorsy and sunny in his subject matter, and the
finest draftsman—the only one whose pencil and charcoal drawings rank,
in their delicate precision and firm roundedness, with those of the Renaissance. He studied under a disciple of Ingres, Louis Lamothe, and copied
masterworks not only as a student but throughout his artistic life; of the
young men who became the Impressionists, he was the least rebellious, in
relation both to his haut-bourgeois family and to the traditional art preserved in the European museums.

Degas has been cast, in the docudrama of art history, as the memori-
alizer of certain beloved, incessantly posterized subjects—ballet dancers
and bathing women foremost, with horses and milliners affectionate also-
rans. The visitor, however, to the huge Degas retrospective that New
York's Metropolitan Museum of Art has established in twelve of its galleries (after showings earlier in 1988 in Paris and Ottawa) will have a long

HILAIRE GERMAIN EDGAR DEGAS
*M. and Mme. Edmondo
Morbilli*, c. 1865
Oil on canvas, 45⅞ × 34¾"
Museum of Fine Arts, Boston
Gift of Robert Treat Paine II

slog before he comes to something easy to love. There was a thick cocoon of umbrageous caution and prickly intelligence that this particular butterfly had to wriggle out of.

The first galleries contain meticulous student sketches and those first whiffs of the peculiar Degas perfume, his early family portraits, including several studies of himself wearing a low-brimmed hat and a translucent mask of shadow. Unlike Rembrandt, he did not go on to record his face at every life-stage; he stopped in his twenties. But he continued to paint the members of his large family, which had branches in Naples and New Orleans, and his own dark heavy-lidded eyes and plump lips echo through their faces. His large painting of his aunt Laura Bellelli with her husband and two daughters, and the joint portrait of his sister Thérèse Morbilli and her husband are among Degas's somber masterpieces, memorable not least for the suggestion of domestic unease and estrangement that infects the slightly unsettled poses. Both paintings achieve their beauty almost entirely in neutral tints—the Morbillis are all gray and dark brown, with even the flesh tones subdued and deathly, and a big central spill of dark-

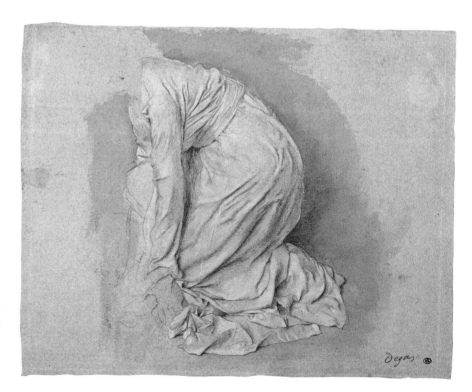

DEGAS
Drapery, study for *Semiramis Building Babylon,* c. 1860–62
Pencil and watercolor heightened with white gouache on gray-blue paper, 9⅝ × 12¼"
Cabinet des Dessins, Musée du Louvre, Paris

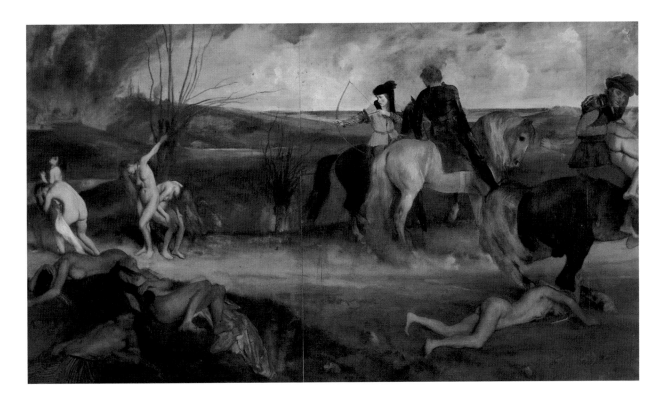

ness dominates the Bellelli group, stark against the white of the girl's aprons and the blue-green of the wallpaper. This blue-green seems, as it ranges in his work from a soft aqua to an incandescent turquoise, a trace of Degas's soul, the one color that he loved.

The early rooms contain a number of ambitious salon-pieces, addressing subjects from myth and history; through these paintings we can feel the blood ebbing from nineteenth-century academic painting. If not absolutely lifeless, *The Daughter of Jephthah* and *Semiramis Building Babylon* are certainly stilted, with their jigsaw pieces of "local color" in the pre-Impressionist style and their populous events inscrutably swathed in antiquity. *Semiramis* occasioned some of Degas's finest drawings—pencil and watercolor studies of draped female forms, each fold scrupulously explored—and prophesied trends to come in his work by containing a well-anatomized horse and by grouping most of its figures tightly in the center of the wide canvas, like people in a transparent elevator. *Scene of War in the Middle Ages,* his last attempt at historical painting, is a work of

DEGAS
Scene of War in the Middle Ages, c. 1863–65
Essence on several pieces of paper joined and mounted on canvas, 31 7/8 × 57 7/8"
Musée d'Orsay, Paris

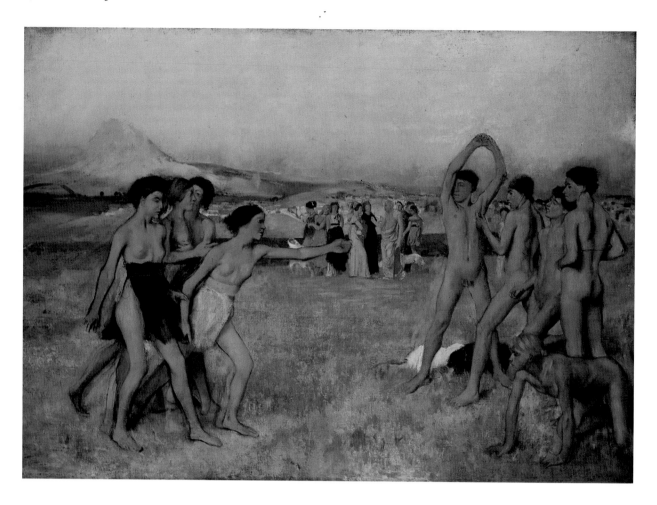

DEGAS
Young Spartans, 1860–62,
reworked until 1880
Oil on canvas, 42⅞ × 61″
The Trustees of the National
Gallery, London

monstrous strangeness, illustrating no known happening but venting the artist's desire to show a number of female nudes in contorted poses, being cruelly slain as they are by an androgynous medieval bowman who, in a preliminary sketch, has breasts. The work seems psychologically as well as visually repellent, and it is something of a triumph of sublimation that the slain females return, ennobled though still contorted, as the pastel bathing women of later decades. Among the historical paintings, only *Young Spartans* is painless to look at, savoring as it so nakedly does of the studio: the brown young bodies, surrounded by a vague and shadowless outdoors, crouch and stretch purely for the benefit of the artist, who has left a number of legs in double outline. The painting was dear to Degas, and he kept it prominently displayed in his studio and worked at it off and

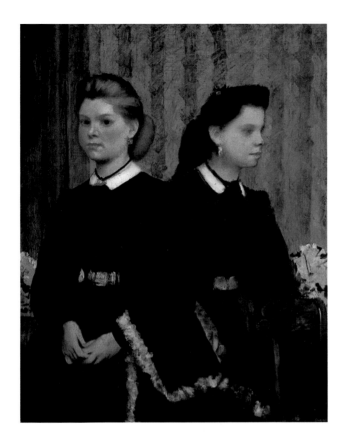

DEGAS
Giovanna and Giulia Bellelli,
1862–64
Oil on canvas, 36¼ × 28½"
The Los Angeles County
Museum of Art. Mr. and Mrs.
George Gard de Sylva Collection

on for twenty years. He was an incorrigible retoucher. He complained that an oil painting is never finished, and in one instance took back a pastel from a buyer, Henri Rouart, and ruined it with revision; Rouart, the story went about Paris, chained to the wall for safekeeping the painting that Degas supplied in restitution.

An unevenness of rendering sometimes betrays Degas's restless methods; in his portrait of his Bellelli cousins, for instance, Giulia exists on a much ghostlier plane than Giovanna, as if a Redon and a Gainsborough shared the same canvas. And in the admired painting from the same mid-1860s, *Woman Leaning near a Vase of Flowers,* the flowers are painstakingly searched out, petal by petal, by another hand than that which casually dashes off the woman, her blurred gaze and sketchy brown dress front. The *Racehorses* of 1875–78 was reworked to the point where no single atmosphere encloses the superimposed figures, and we seem to be underwater. Degas was a fusser, a *bricoleur,* a studio assembler of effects. Even those works of his that seem most spontaneous and on-the-spot, the monotypes of brothels, had to be, from their technical nature, studio artifacts, and are unreal in their ubiquitous nudity and lack of individualization. A dramatic image like *The Song of the Dog* was worked up with gouache and pastel over a monotype base, and the paper was enlarged by the addition of strips—a frequent Degas refinement. In *Dancers in the Wing* ten separate bits of paper have been counted.

His most brilliant and characteristic achievement might be described as the patient invention of the snapshot, before the camera itself was technically able to arrest motion and record the poetry of visual accident. Equipped with a collage of sketches and the compositional example of Japanese prints, he began, in the early 1870s, to make pictures truly novel in their off-center foci, the cropping action of their edges, their unexpected points of vantage and dramatic perspectives, the electric violence of their lighting. The discovery of stage lighting, as a means of organizing a painting, effectuated an intensification of his vision, favoring his virtuoso draftsmanship and reducing color to a matter of highlights. In *The Orchestra of the Opéra,* the orchestra in the foreground is a dark mass of naturalistic portraits—each musician personally identifiable—and the background of actual performance is impressionistically splashed across the top, the dancers dissolved in light and cut off at their necks. *The Ballet from "Robert le Diable"* uses the same scheme: a lot is happening in the overlapped silhouettes of audience and orchestra—one man is tilting his opera glasses upward, another man is blowing the stem of his oboe—while on the stage blurred white forms, out of focus in paint, are staging a crisis. This slanted staginess, this multi-angled jumble of differently directed energies, not only animates the gaudy magic of the famous ballet pastels but supplies the nervous energy in the paintings of jockeys and horses and in such active interior scenes as *The Song Rehearsal* and, in more stately fashion, *Portraits in an Office,* with its cast of fourteen different men engaged in the cotton trade. The murderous arrows of Degas's medieval scene of war have become the darting vectors of overdirected modern attention.

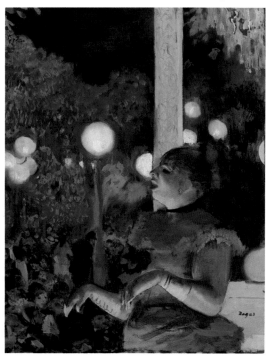

DEGAS
The Song of the Dog,
c. 1876–77
Gouache and pastel over
monotype on three joined pieces
of paper, 22 5/8 × 17 1/8″
Private collection

(Opposite) DEGAS
*The Ballet from
"Robert le Diable,"* 1871
Oil on canvas, 26 × 21 3/8″
The Metropolitan Museum
of Art, New York. Bequest of
Mrs. H. O. Havemeyer, 1929.
The H. O. Havemeyer Collection

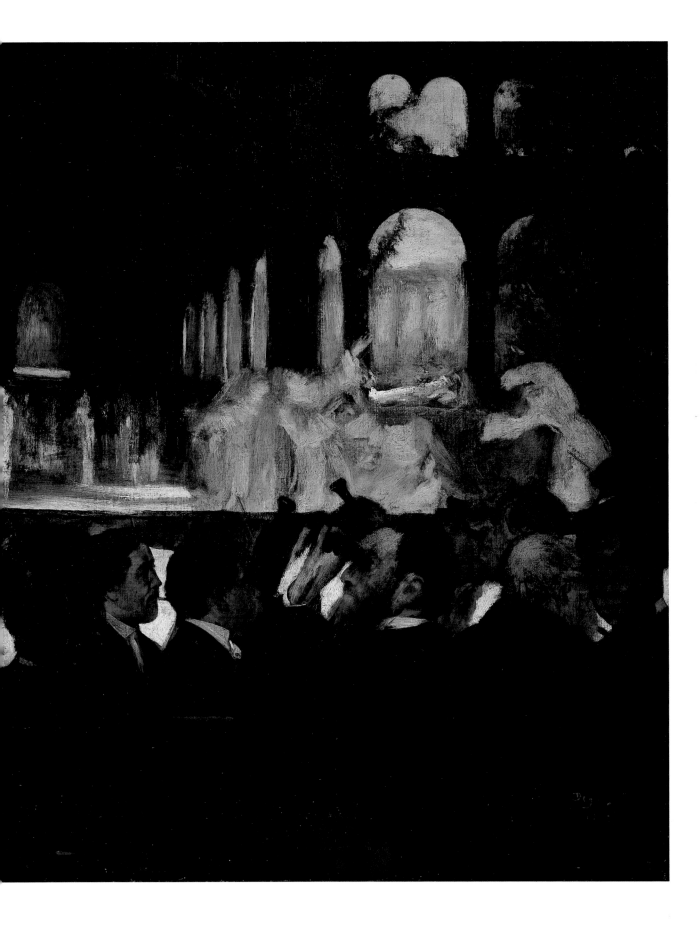

As the viewer makes his way through the middle galleries of this show, where Degas's cunning theatricality asserts itself, he becomes aware not only of the figures on display but, with a strange intensity, the rooms. *Portraits in an Office* presents a thorough inventory of the shelves, chairs, and windowed partitions of a New Orleans business office; *The Song Rehearsal* defines with an architectural clarity the moldings and trim of its large chamber; the stately bare walls of *The Dance Class* in its

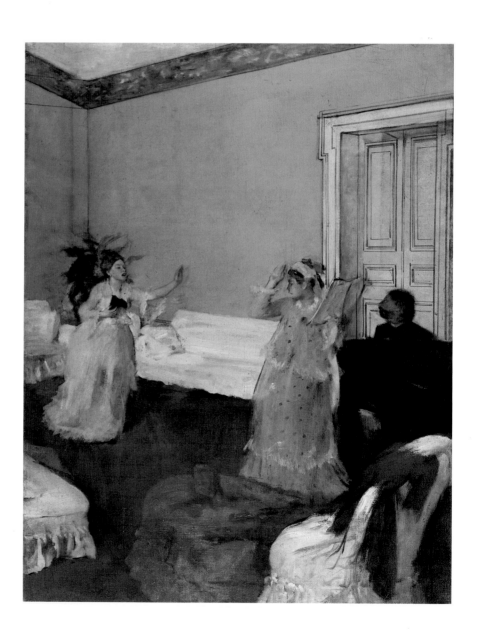

DEGAS
The Song Rehearsal, 1872–73
Oil on canvas, 3 1 7/8 × 2 5 5/8″
Dumbarton Oaks Research
Library and Collection,
Washington, D.C.

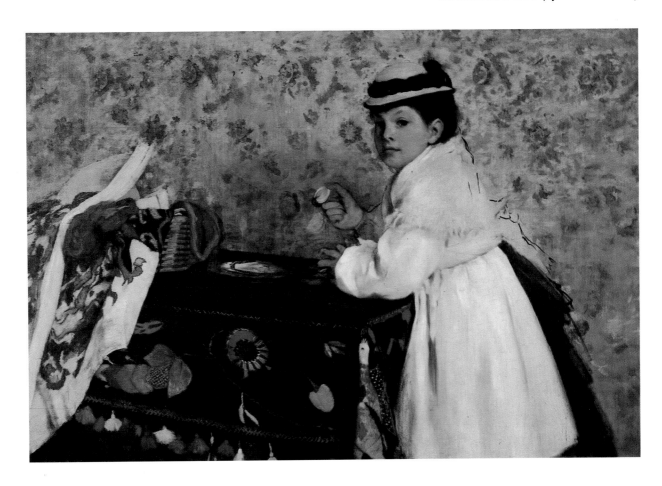

several versions cast a palpable, somewhat desolating atmosphere; and a slightly earlier painting like the enigmatic *Interior* makes the room—whose odd immensity is left unfilled by its slender furniture and two preoccupied inhabitants—the main presence. In more intimate works like *The Pedicure* and *Hortense Valpinçon* the furniture and wallpaper mingle with the young female subjects in the forefront of our attention. The environment, we are subtly invited to understand, is part of the picture, and with the same subtlety Degas's paintings of laundresses and milliners and entertainers imply an enveloping society, a world of work and display. His social realism disdains glamorization and also pity, of the kind that Daumier's paintings of the working class invoked. Degas's whores are fat women well past first bloom, stolid and bored in their trade, and his ballet dancers are bony girls, professional or studying to be, drooping with fa-

DEGAS
Mlle. Hortense Valpinçon, Enfant, 1871
Oil on canvas, 30 × 43 5/8″
The Minneapolis Institute of Arts. The John R. Van Derlip Fund

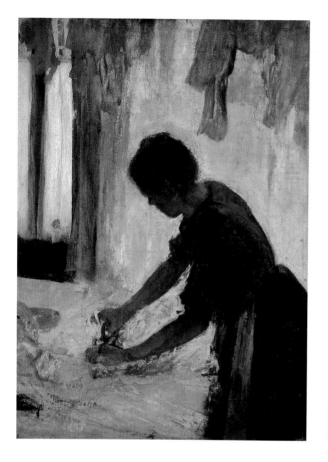

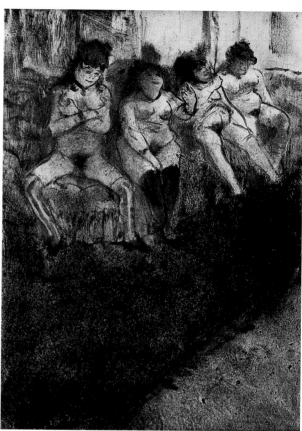

DEGAS
(Left) *A Woman Ironing*, c. 1873
Oil on canvas, 21 3/8 × 15 1/2″
The Metropolitan Museum
of Art, New York. Bequest of
Mrs. H. O. Havemeyer, 1929
The H. O. Havemeyer Collection

(Right) *Waiting*
(second version), 1879
Monotype in black ink on
China paper, plate 8 1/2 × 6 1/2″
Musée Picasso, Paris

tigue offstage and helplessly yawning. He catches them in awkward moments, just as he likes to show, in little wax statues, horses rearing awkwardly, in off-balance poses that can have been maintained for less than a
second. There is in Degas a democracy of vision that gives the awkward
and the ugly equal representation with the graceful and beautiful; he anticipated a camera's capabilities in his cropped and eclipsed assemblages
and also its dispassion, its acceptance of what it sees. This acceptance is
more sociologically flavored than the acceptance of riverine shimmer that
inspired the free and broken brushwork of Monet and Renoir the summer
(1869) they painted side by side at La Grenouillère, and Impressionism
crystallized. Though he exhibited with the "Impressionists"—so named
by a headline writer for *Le Charivari*, titling an unfavorable review by
Louis Leroy that singled out Monet's *Impression: Sunrise*—from their

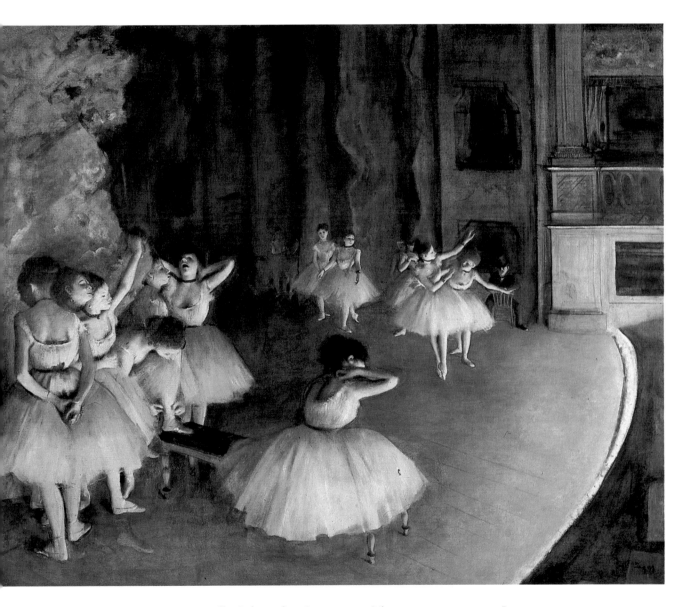

Degas   *Ballet Rehearsal on Stage,* 1874. Oil on canvas, 25 5/8 × 31 7/8″
Musée d'Orsay, Paris

first group show in 1874 to their last in 1886, Degas was painting masterly portraits while Monet was still a truant art student. The Impressionist revolution had in detached, reactionary Degas its humanist, the least didactic of social observers.

The leg-weary traverser of the twelve grand Metropolitan galleries will encounter by mid-journey celebrated examples of Degas's charm—*The Green Dancer,* seen from above, her tulle skirt spread in apotheosis of that pet blue-green color; *The Little Fourteen-Year-Old Dancer,* the most winsome of unforgettable statues—but he must wait until Gallery Nine for splendor. Degas's large pastel studies of women bathing were, we are told, the sensation of the last Impressionist exhibition, and sociologically they reflected a general increase of private bathrooms in the middle-class home. This scrupulous realist found the perfect modern excuse for the female nude, which hitherto was encountered in mythology, which had become ridiculous, or in lovemaking, which was indecent. Bathing created a third occasion when women took off their clothes, and artists before Degas had seized upon it. But Titian's bather is Venus, arising from the sea, and in Renoir the bathing beauty is still glazed by a goddesslike glow and immobility, posed pink against the timeless Mediterranean. Degas's bathers are splendid by virtue only of the forms God gave them and the vivacious, glowing pastels in which Degas renders them. Chalk on paper has a slight graininess that answers to the texture of skin; his paintings of bathers are not quite so alive, though even bigger in scale. He shows the women—hired models, and not, as in Bonnard's case, a consort who happened to bathe a lot—stepping into a tub, stepping out into a towel held by a servant, stooping to scrub or dry their feet, squatting and sponging the back of their necks. The poses are angular and sometimes awkward, but even when a stooped-over position thrusts the buttocks at us the representation's sexual content remains submissive to the larger natural fact that this is an animal body cleansing and grooming itself, in an atmosphere of silence and peace, of private holiday. The bodies verge on plumpness; the plumpest of them, in *The Morning Bath,* was later nicknamed *La Boulangère (The Baker's Wife).* These magnificent apparitions are always tied, by the tubs and pitchers and towels around them, to settings of homely middle-class domesticity. Degas, who never married and kept no known mistress, was thought, by Manet among others, to be impotent; but these bathing women excited him. His excitement shows in the freedom and variety of his color; in the strength of his line, thicker but

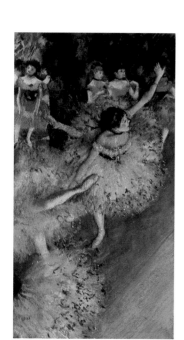

DEGAS
The Green Dancer, c. 1880
Pastel and gouache on heavy wove paper, 26 × 14¼″
Copyright © Museo Thyssen-Bornemisza, Madrid

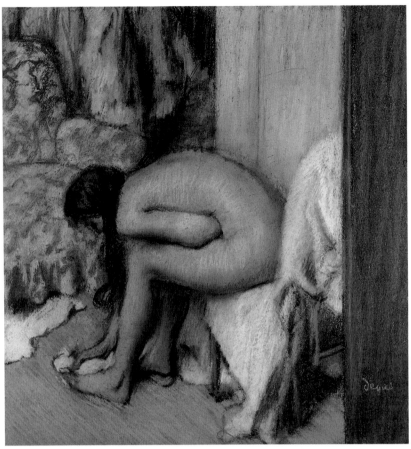

DEGAS (Above) *Nude Woman Drying Her Foot*, c. 1885–86
Pastel on buff heavy wove paper, 21 3/8 × 20 5/8". Musée d'Orsay, Paris

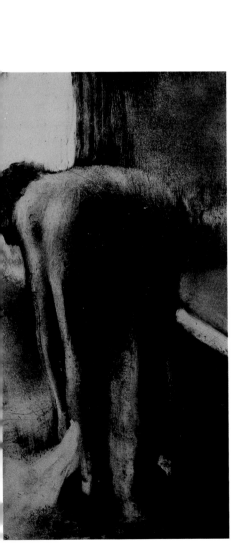

(Left) *Nude Woman Wiping Her Feet*, c. 1879–83
Monotype in black ink on cream-colored heavy laid paper,
plate 17 3/4 × 9 3/8". Cabinet des Dessins, Musée du Louvre, Paris

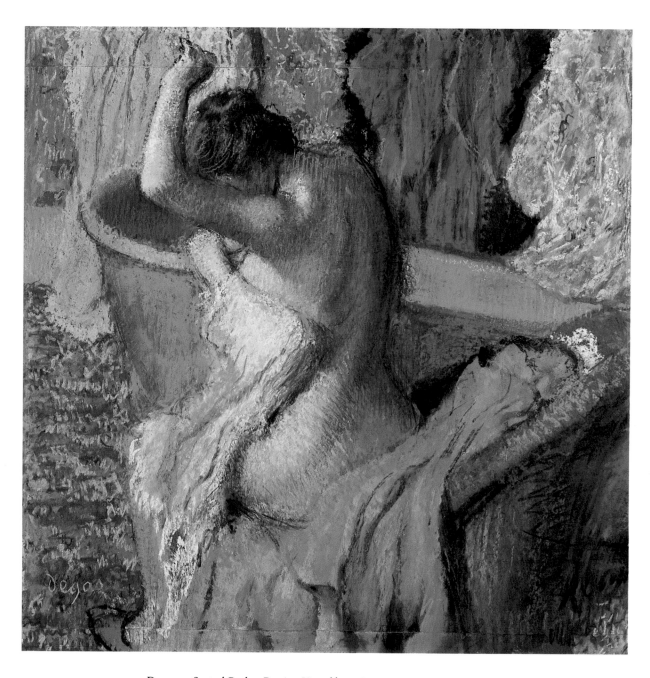

DEGAS   *Seated Bather Drying Herself*, c. 1895
Pastel on wove paper, with strips added to top and bottom, 20½ × 20½"
Collection of Bob and Kathy Guccione

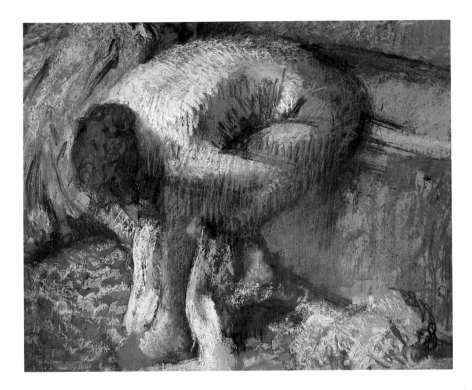

DEGAS
*Nude Woman Drying
Her Feet*, c. 1895
Pastel, 18 1/8 × 23 1/4"
Collection of Muriel and Philip
Berman, Allentown, Pennsylvania

no less elegant than that of Ingres; in the rapacious vigor and variety of his strokes, which in some of the later nudes, from the mid-1890s—one drying her feet and another lying on her stomach—show as scribbles and furious parallel rows that resolve into skin tint only at a significant distance. *Seated Bather Drying Herself* is perhaps the most splendid of all, her back twisted half into shadow and plunged into a nest of clothy patches of color. In a virtual expressionist fury Degas began to steam and melt his pastels, and to press them into a chalky impasto, and to etch the thickened surface with knives and needles.

As his eyes increasingly dimmed, Degas perforce experimented with roughness of execution, never losing his underlying integrity of drawing. The portrait of Rose Caron is almost faceless, yet reads as a real presence. Some of his colored monotypes called landscapes are amazingly abstract. Only in the *Russian Dancers* series of 1899 did he reach beyond, for me, the useful limits of violence. Taking tracings of the same pose of wideskirted Russian dancers, like pages of a coloring book, he filled in the

DEGAS
Russian Dancers, 1899
Pastel on paper, 24½ × 24¾″
The Museum of Fine Arts,
Houston. Gift of Audrey
Jones Beck

outlines as if in a jubilant return to the local color of the academic tradition, and produced coarsely decorative images that seem brave but little else. They suggest Monet's wildly chromatic studies of haystacks and cathedral fronts, with the difference that Monet was working from nature and actual light, where Degas was returning to the studio of imagination, which in the coming century would again dominate the painter's art.

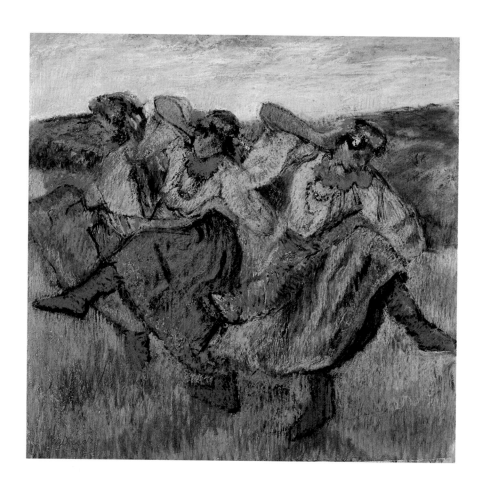

Some Rectangles of Blue

———

THE WRITTEN WORD, and the mode of thinking that words shape, still stand embarrassed before abstract art. What is it *about*? What is *happening*? The artists, quite rightly, spurn verbal explaining, claiming paint to be a sufficient vocabulary. However, some, like Barnett Newman, have been formidable theorizers and articulators of theory; indeed, none have been without some weaponry of programmatic thought, so deeply entrenched is our (and their) expectation of the representational, and so recently has it been overthrown. Though abstract design has figured in primitive art since its beginnings, and Mondrian and Malevich perpetrated, on opposite sides of Europe, the first purely abstract paintings as long ago as this century's second decade, it was not until the birth of Action Painting and its rapid triumph in the New York of the late Forties and Fifties that abstraction swept all before it. Even then, there were ghosts of subject matter—survivals in Pollock's drip paintings of the themes of mythic sacrifice and violence that had concerned him earlier, hints in Kline's big black slashes of the black and white of his youthful cartooning, a certain floating Jewish mysticism in the canvases of Rothko and Newman. In 1944 Robert Motherwell wrote of his friend Jackson Pollock, "His principal problem is to discover what his true subject is. And since painting is his thought's medium, the resolution must grow out of the process of his painting itself." Three years later, in sudden full

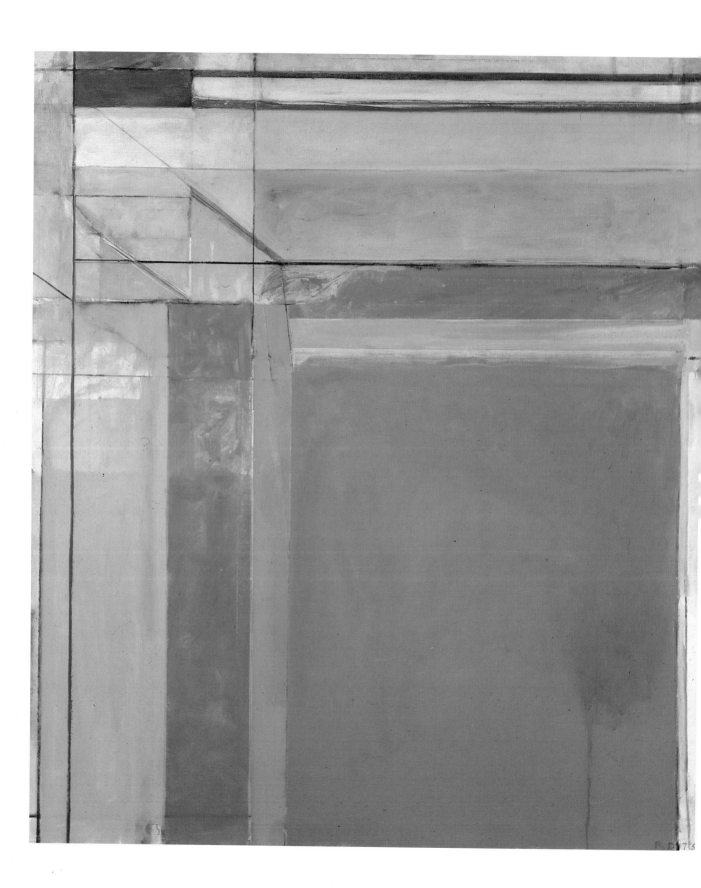

stride, Pollock could state, "When I am *in* my painting, I'm not aware of what I'm doing." Pollock painting is the subject of Pollock's paintings. Abstract Expressionism has the effect of glamorizing the painter, of making him, rather than the sitter or the landscape or the Virgin, the star.

We are here in the presence of a Diebenkorn, of Diebenkorn. He first achieved notice as a member of the West Coast "neo-figurative" school, but has returned to big abstract paintings, as to a new classic tradition. This painting has a title, *Ocean Park No. 79*, and we greedily seize on the "ocean," linking it with the dominant blue. Yet the ocean (if that is what it is) seems to be in the foreground, and what might be a strip of sandy beach is at the top. We feel, for a moment, amid all these spindly horizontals and verticals, inside a beach house, looking out of a big window at the sea. But no, that won't do, the blue is too resolutely paint, flat and rather thin, with scrub marks and even a dribble showing, and the linear elements create no space that would house us. Yet the sensation of ocean persists, a placidity and breadth viewed from some distance, on a quiet, even a dull, day.

The painting in reality measures eight feet by seven. Our reproduction is eleven times smaller, and perhaps deceives us into pictorial speculations. Turning the pages of a book or magazine, we expect meaning; but in an actual environment, a museum or an opulent home, we settle for thereness. Abstraction removes painting from the secondary realm of imitation and enrolls it in the primary order of mute objects. That is its genius and its susceptibility. Meeting a painting like this, so beautiful in its balanced tones and enigmatic nervousness, not in our reductive pages but on a suitably large wall, we accept it as "art," an expensive variety of wallpaper. Inarticulate but unembarrassed, we pass on, as if the canvas has said to us, "Have a nice day."

RICHARD DIEBENKORN
Ocean Park No. 79, 1975
Oil on canvas, 93 × 81″
Philadelphia Museum of Art
Purchased with a grant from the
National Endowment for the
Arts and with funds contributed
by private donors

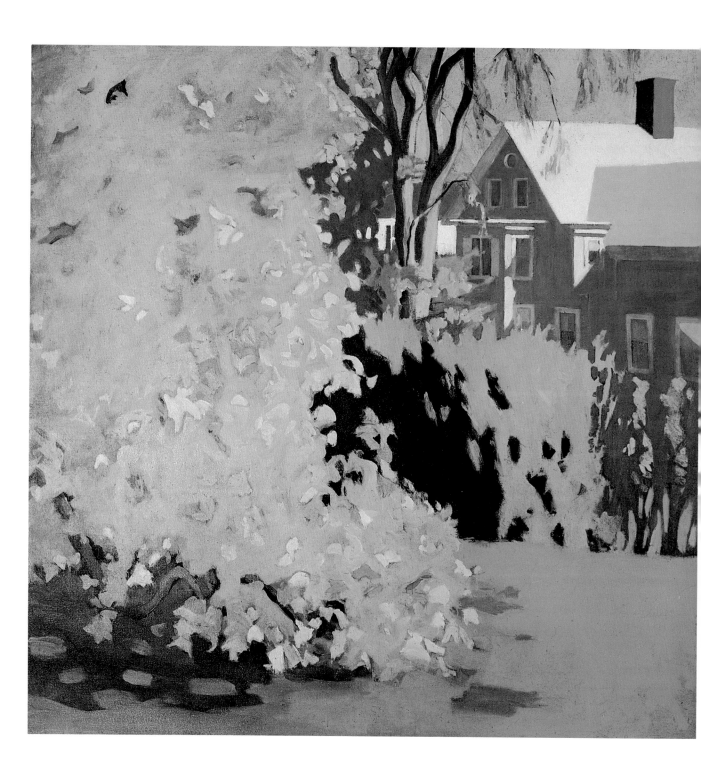

Violence at the Windows

———

REPRESENTATIONAL painting asks a double response from the viewer: to the subject depicted and to the manner of depiction, of painting. One of the delights of the 1983 show "Fairfield Porter: Realist Painter in an Age of Abstraction," one hundred forty-four works assembled by the Boston Museum of Fine Arts' curator of twentieth-century art, Kenworth Moffett, surely lay, for many visitors, in its frank and sunny rendering of sights and scenes familiar to the well-to-do of the Northeast coast. Porter, son of a wealthy Chicago family, studied fine arts at Harvard and after graduation in 1928 moved to New York and attended the Art Students League for two years. He travelled in Europe, flirted with socialism, lived in Westchester, owned a town house on Fifty-second Street, and finally in 1949 settled in Southampton, Long Island, where he lived except in the summer, when he took his family to a vacation house his father had designed in Great Spruce Head, Maine. Porter and his wife, Anne (née Channing, from Boston), had, all told, five children, and their solemn-eyed heads and rather wooden figures adorn a great number of his canvases. He painted what he saw, and what he saw were the isles and evergreens and rocky harbors of Maine; the large homes and lush lawns and massy elms and hedges and flowering shrubs of the Hamptons; beaches and the sea; children and guests on the screened porch; tables set for breakfast or with arrangements of flowers; and big, bright rooms

FAIRFIELD PORTER
Columbus Day, 1968
Oil on canvas, 80 × 80″
Courtesy Hirschl & Adler
Galleries, New York

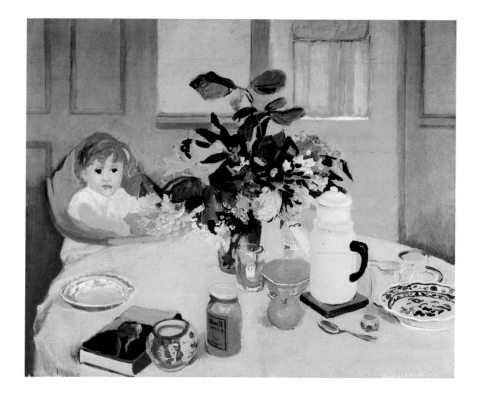

brimming with possessions, not the claustrophobic furnishings of the old rich but the dishevelled plenty of their vaguely bohemian offspring, who seem to live in summer houses all year long. Nice people, nice places, pleasantly redolent of affection and sensitivity and, that great underwriter of both, money.

Money, too, underwrote Fairfield Porter's dedicated hours at the easel, pursuing techniques and artistic ideals that at no point from 1938 (the date of the oldest painting in the show) to 1975 (the year of his death) could have been called fashionable. His hero was Edouard Vuillard; he regarded everyone from Cézanne on as betrayers of Impressionism. He studied at the Art Students League with Thomas Hart Benton and Boardman Robinson; he thought Benton a bad painter and a "tiresome" teacher, Robinson a better teacher but no good as a painter. The famous Armory show he considered "a complete disaster to American art," deepening this art's provinciality. His dislikes ranged widely, from Arshile Gorky to Andrew Wyeth. But he liked Joseph Cornell's boxes. As an art critic for *The Nation* and *Art News* he coped sympathetically with Abstract Expressionism in its heyday and knew everybody, being especially close to the de Koonings and such members of the post-Pollock generation as Alex Katz, Jane Freilicher, Neil Welliver, and Larry Rivers. It is hard not to feel, reading the forewords that Mr. Moffett and John Ashbery have written for the catalogue, that this earnest, cranky rich man's son was a bit patronized in the heady art circles of Manhattan and its exurban enclaves. Saul Steinberg once asked him at a party if he painted the way he did for political reasons. Clement Greenberg told him he was conceited and that "you can't paint figuratively today." Those gallery managers who, from the early 1950s on, often at the urging of more "in" artists like de Kooning and Jack Tworkov, gave Porter some wall space could hardly in their fondest dreams have foreseen so augustly extensive a one-man show.

Less might have been more. There are perhaps six superb paintings and two dozen more that well reward contemplation. The rest are tainted to a greater or lesser degree by a quality one might call amateurism, were not so many supreme twentieth-century artists amateurs in the financial sense. Faces gave Porter a lot of trouble, and his paint thickens as he worries at them. His still lifes of flowers tend to be garish and flaky in the classic Sunday-painter manner. Some of his paintings are so sharp in color they look better dulled in reproduction. Sometimes he was hasty; notice, for example, the schematic hinges, cartooned in red monochrome, at the vertical center of *Door to the Woods*. His impressionism, in such a work as the 1968 *Self-portrait*, approaches the facile dashingness of magazine illustration. He was a considerable user of raw white—the caked spreads of it in *Sun Rising Out of the Mist* and *Blue Sunrise* give a flat effect the opposite of atmospheric. There was something ingenuous about Porter's belief that the appearance of anything could be reduced to paint. *The Fire* attempts to make a still-life subject of a log blaze in the fireplace, flames, andirons, and all. His several studies of oncoming waves seen from a beach look more like hummocks in a giant earthworks than any fusion of wind and water. In paintings like these he seems primitive. A visit to the Boston museum's lower level, where a complementary show of such contemporary realists as Welliver, George Nick, David Park, and

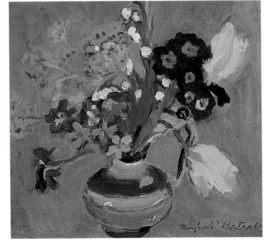

PORTER
Flowers to the Background, 1965
Oil on Masonite, 8 × 9″
Courtesy Hirschl & Adler
Galleries, New York

(Opposite) PORTER
Interior with a Dress Pattern, 1969
Oil on canvas, 62 × 46"
Collection of Mr. and Mrs. Austin List

Lennart Anderson has been assembled, reveals how much, as far as technique goes, Porter had to learn.

Yet in his best work, which tends to be that of his last ten years, his stubbornness and fidelity did bring off a miracle: an Intimism with an American spaciousness, a color-drunk hymn to (in his phrase) "things as they are." The blue sea caught in the screened rectangles of *Still Life with White Boats* looks crude by itself but takes a key place in an alignment of blues that frames light and space. *Interior with a Dress Pattern,* the most closely worked painting in the show, describes a domestic interior so lovingly that the viewer feels invited to come in and take a chair; its range of reds and dark golds compares with the sumptuous calm of Matisse's *Red Studio* and Piero della Francesca's stately explorations of perspective. *Island Farmhouse* and *Boathouses and Lobster Pots* are more reductive, like silk screens in their cut-out shapes and limited palettes, with a distilled intensity in certain details—the dog at rest in the sloping green shadow, the yellow shadows of clapboards, the boats the exact same gray as their shadows in the mist, the suspended scraps of cloud and sky.

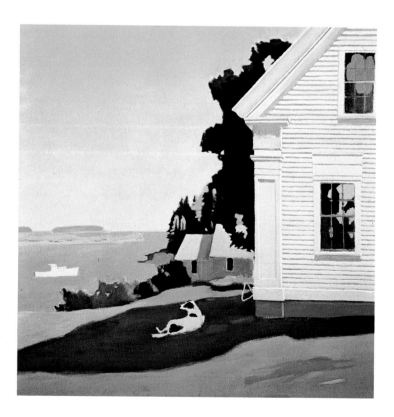

PORTER
Island Farmhouse, 1969
Oil on canvas, 797/8 × 791/2"
Private collection

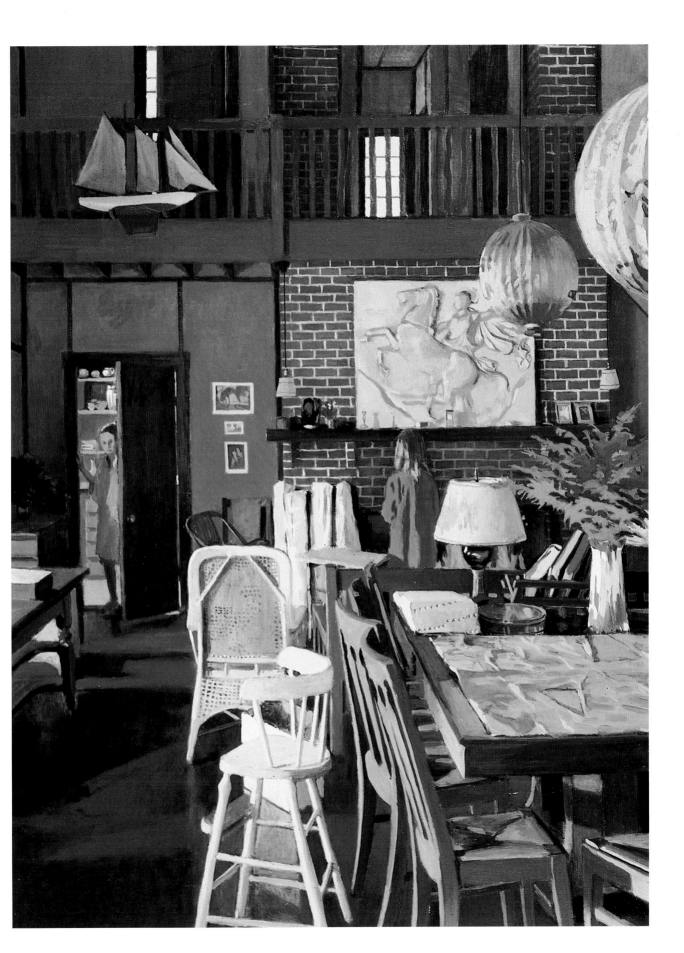

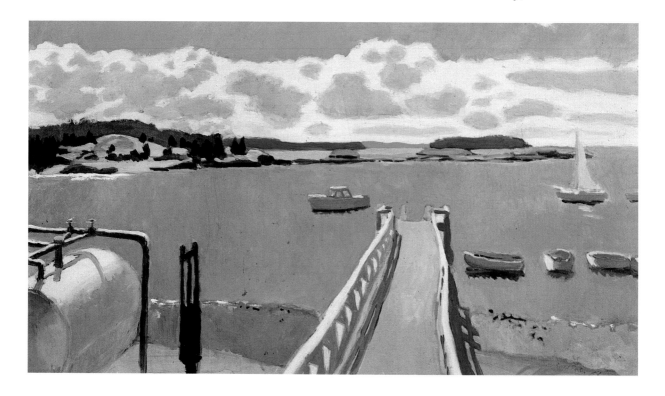

PORTER
The Harbor—Great Spruce
Head Island, 1974
Oil on canvas, 20 × 36"
Private collection

Clouds—clouds as they actually are—became one of Porter's strong suits; where else but in *The Harbor—Great Spruce Head* have we seen painted those leaden lavender cores at the heart of radiant cumulus? From the Abstract Expressionists Porter learned boldness, the boldness of broad monochrome expanses and of loaded brushstrokes. Often he defines a tree's structure by slashing into its mass with daubs of the background color. Sunlight explodes with terrific violence at the windows of his hushed interiors. In *Cliffs of Isle au Haut* (a canvas that seems to borrow some of the color-by-number texture of Welliver's landscapes), a spiky blob as opaquely black as anything in Kline or Motherwell overspreads the foreground without "reading" as the natural phenomenon it undoubtedly was. The two children's heads peeping over the lichenous rocks restore us, however, to Porter's domestic world.

Moving through the galleries, one becomes aware of what Porter deliberately does not do. He does not, unlike Nick and Hopper, offer any elegiac, generalized statement about American architecture or the lay of our

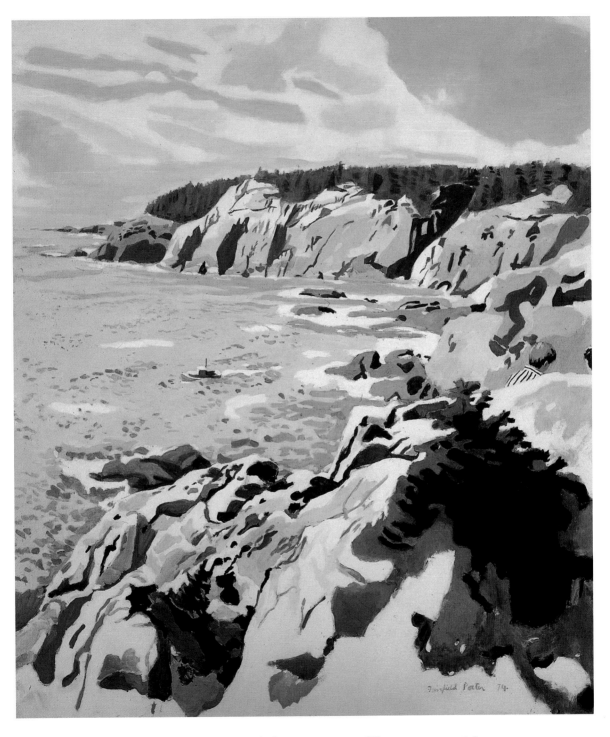

PORTER   *The Cliffs of Isle au Haut,* 1974. Oil on canvas, 72×62″
Courtesy Hirschl & Adler Galleries, New York

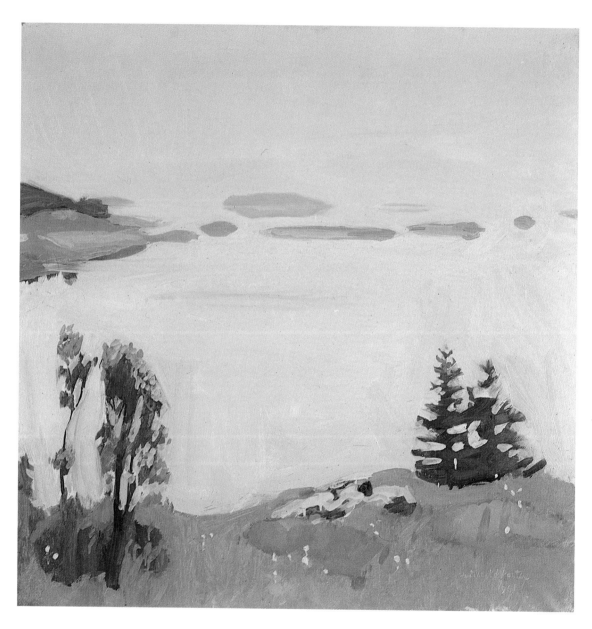

PORTER   *Calm Morning*, 1961. Oil on canvas, 36 × 36″
Collection of Arthur M. Bullowa

land. Nor is any psychological mood being struck, such as the dramatic loneliness of Hopper's figures or the glittering menace of Richard Estes's depopulated streets. One exception is *Door to the Woods,* where the woodsy tangle surges toward the door's frame like a caged beast. *Under the Elms* has a Munch-like morbidity, and a frozen heaviness attends many of the portraits; but this burden may be less projected by the painter than undischarged by him. Usually the pleasant environment of Fairfield Porter seems what he wanted it to be: an occasion for rendering color. As a colorist he attained some triumphs that transcend subject matter. The painting itself—where, say, the distant islands of *Calm Morning* float as mere oblong brushstrokes on a field of lilac gray—becomes emotion, and our response becomes one not merely of recognition but of discovery.

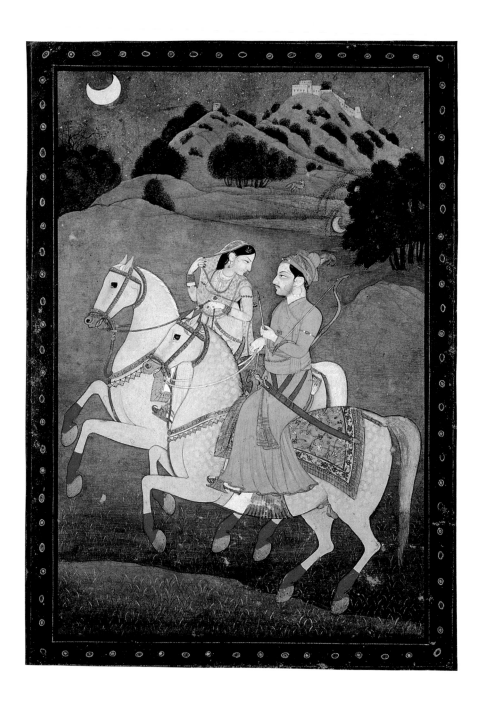

Moving Along

———

IN DREAMS, one is frequently travelling, and the more hallucinatory moments of our waking life, many of them, are spent in cars, trains, and airplanes. For millennia, Man has walked or run to where he wanted to go; the first naked ape who had the mad idea of mounting a horse (or was it a *Camelops?*) launched a series of subtle internal dislocations of which jet lag is a vivid modern form. When men come to fly through space at near the speed of light, they will return to earth a century later but only a few years older. Now, driving (say) from Boston to Pittsburgh in a day, we arrive feeling greatly aged by the engine's innumerable explosive heart-beats, by the monotony of the highway surface and the constant windy press of unnatural speed. Beside the highway, a clamorous parasitic life signals for attention and halt; localities where generations have lived, bred, labored, and died are flung through the windshield and out through the rearview mirror. Men on the move brutalize themselves and render the world they arrow through phantasmal.

Our two artists, separated by two centuries, capture well the eeriness of travel. In the Punjab Hills painting, Baz Bahadur, prince of Malwa, has eloped with the lovely Rupmati; in order to keep him faithful to her, the legend goes, she takes him riding by moonlight. The moon appears to exist not only in the sky but behind a grove of trees. Deer almost blend into the mauve-gray hills. A little citadel basks in starlight on a hilltop. In

Artist unknown
Baz Bahadur and Rupmati Riding by Moonlight, c. 1780
Pahari miniature in Kangra style, 8³/₄ × 6¹/₄"
The British Museum, Department of Oriental Antiquities, London

this soft night, nothing is brighter than the scarlet pasterns of the horses. Baz Bahadur's steed bears on his hide a paler version of the starry sky, and in his violet genitals carries a hint of this nocturnal ride's sexual undercurrent. To judge from the delicacy of their gestures and glances, the riders are being borne along as smoothly as on a merry-go-round. Though these lovers and their panoply are formalized to static perfection, if we cover them, a surprising depth appears in the top third of the painting, and carries the eye away.

The riders in Roy de Forest's contemporary painting move through a forest as crowded, garish, and menacing as the neon-lit main drag of a city. A throng of sinister bystanders, one built of brick and another with

ROY DE FOREST
Canoe of Fate, 1974
Polymer on canvas,
66³/₄ × 90¹/₄″
Philadelphia Museum of Art
The Adele Haas Turner and
Beatrice Pastorius Turner Fund

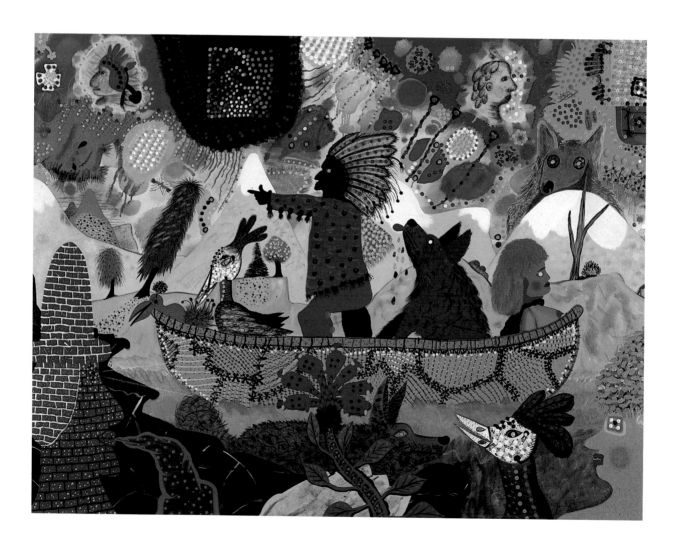

eyes that are paste gems, witness the passage of this *Canoe of Fate,* which with the coarseness of its stitching and the bulk of its passengers would make slow headway even on a less crowded canvas. Beyond the mountains, heavenly medallions and balloons of stippled color pre-empt space. Only the gesture of the black brave, echoing that of George Washington in another fabulous American crossing, gives a sense of direction and promises to open a path. Two exotic birds, a slavering wolf, and what may be a fair captive (gazing backward toward settlements where other red-haired bluefaces mourn her) freight the canoe with a suggestion of allegory, of myths to which we have lost the key. The personnel of the aboriginal New World, at any rate, are here deep-dyed but not extinguished by the glitter and jazz of an urban-feeling wilderness.

In both representations, the movement is from right to left, like that of writing in the Semitic languages, like the motion of a mother when she instinctively shifts her baby to her left arm, to hold it closer to her heart. It feels natural, this direction, and slightly uphill. We gaze at these dreamlike tapestries of travel confident that no progress will be made—we will awaken in our beds.

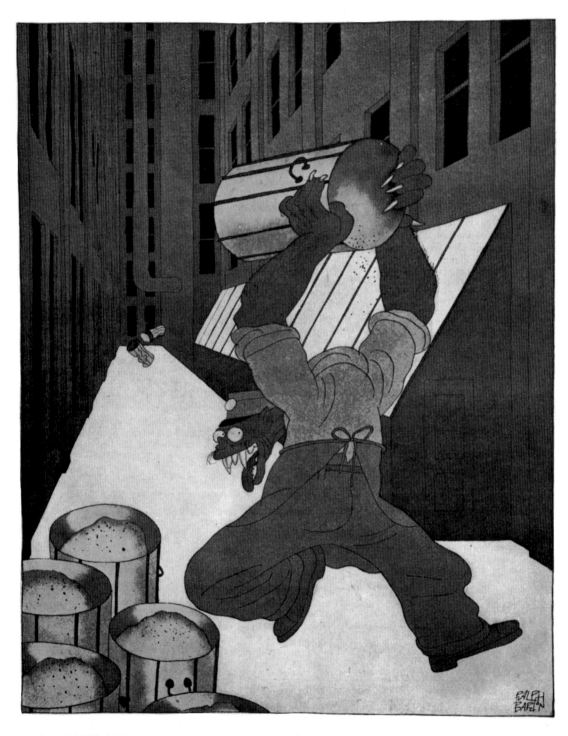

THE SORT OF THING THAT BRINGS JOY TO THE ASHMAN'S BLACK HEART

A WHOLE, NICE, NEW, BIG, TWENTY-STORY, CO-OPERATIVE APARTMENT HOUSE TO WAKE UP
AT SIX IN THE MORNING

A Case of Melancholia

THIS CARTOON, reproduced in the first *New Yorker Album* (1928) and also in *The New Yorker Album of Drawings 1925–1975*, haunts me. As an adolescent cartoon buff, I didn't think it terribly funny, just oddly intense, with something malevolent in the rendering of the ashman's simian limbs, drooping gargoylish head, fangs, pop eyes, and crazily lolling tongue. As a grown man, who has suffered some nights of noisy trash collection in the city of New York, I better appreciate its harsh truth, and the artful way the exaggerated perspective sets off the cacophonous reverberation of those distant hurled cans. The receding walls and darkened windows, as uniform as prison windows, eat up the viewer.

Ralph Barton's drawings, like his signature, have a squared-off quality, a frame of high intention that suggests an aspiration beyond the momentary smile most cartoons are content to induce. A cartoon traditionally aims to give all its information at a glance; it is a kind of calligraphy, which reduces marginal details to the most quickly readable scribble. But in Barton the background presses toward the foreground with an insistence found in Oriental art, and again in Cubism. He undertook for *The New Yorker* a series called *The 1930's*, when that brand-new decade seemed no more than a hungover extension of the 1920s. In *Weekend Guests*, published in August 1930, an extraordinary formality poses the bold triangle of main figures and foreshortens the two sunk in the sofa

RALPH BARTON
Cartoon from
The New Yorker, 1926

into separate body parts—legs, hands, and heads suspended in queasy malaise and surrounded by the geometrical jiggle of the lozenges of the tiles, the squares and ovals of the Sunday rotogravure, the ribs and ripples of the gentleman's country outfit, the overlapping rings of transparency in the lady's glass. Beyond the triangle, in stark and sickening sunlight, three smaller figures slouch doggedly in pursuit of a good outdoor time. The dazed, breeze-teased suffocation of a country weekend—the Sunday stuffy-sofa feeling—finds reinforced expression in the tight-knit stasis of the drawing, its crammed elegance. Barton's pen lines are like wires that are all connected; his drawings give off a peculiar hum, a menace absent from the tidy lines of similar draftsmen like Josef Čapek, Nicolas Bentley, Rea Irvin, Gluyas Williams, and Abner Dean.

Ralph Waldo Emerson Barton was born in Kansas City, Missouri, in August of 1891. His father, Abraham Pool Barton, was a Missouri farm boy, the eldest of eleven children, who put himself through college and law school; in his fifties he gave up his law practice to follow full-time his secondary career as the publisher of a weekly metaphysical journal called *The Life* and as a lecturer on his philosophy of religion and healing. His published books include *The ABC of Truth, being Twenty-six Basic Lessons in the Science of Life; The Bible and Eternal Punishment, Proving from the Original Languages that the Bible does not Teach the Doctrine;* and *Why Are We Here, or the Meaning and Purpose of This Incarnation.* He and his wife were friends and Kansas City neighbors of Mr. and Mrs. Charles Fillmore, the founders of the Unity School of Christianity. Mrs. Barton, née Catherine Josephine Wigginton, was a locally well-known portrait painter and a partner in her husband's religious enterprises; she herself published books expressing her beliefs, with such titles as *The Mother of the Living* and *The Interlude.* Remarkably, she gave birth to Ralph, the youngest of her four children, when she was forty-four, and lived to the age of eighty-eight, surviving all her children but one. In interviews, she claimed that there had been an artist in her family for seven generations, and that since she had found art supplies, including paper, scarce in her girlhood she "made it one of her chief duties to see that her son was plentifully supplied with such things." His mother's studio was Ralph's main art school, though after attending the city's Central High School he briefly studied at the Art Students League in Chicago. He did drawings for both the major Kansas City newspapers, the *Journal-*

BARTON
Cartoon from
The New Yorker, 1930

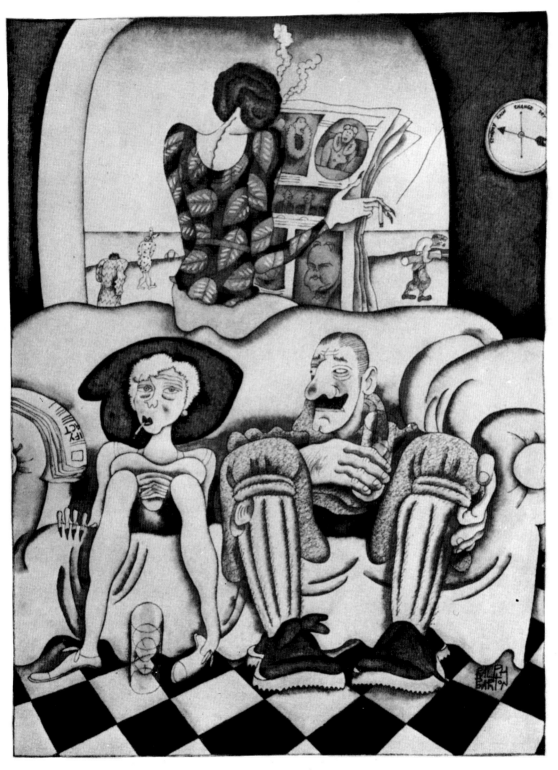

THE 1930'S
Weekend Guests—Sunday Morning after Saturday Night

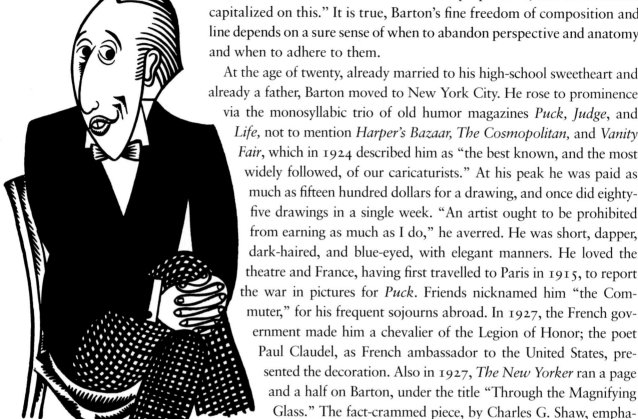

Post and the *Star*. A member of the *Star*'s art department recalled of Barton, "He never could draw in the correct proportions, and he afterward capitalized on this." It is true, Barton's fine freedom of composition and line depends on a sure sense of when to abandon perspective and anatomy and when to adhere to them.

At the age of twenty, already married to his high-school sweetheart and already a father, Barton moved to New York City. He rose to prominence via the monosyllabic trio of old humor magazines *Puck*, *Judge*, and *Life*, not to mention *Harper's Bazaar*, *The Cosmopolitan*, and *Vanity Fair*, which in 1924 described him as "the best known, and the most widely followed, of our caricaturists." At his peak he was paid as much as fifteen hundred dollars for a drawing, and once did eighty-five drawings in a single week. "An artist ought to be prohibited from earning as much as I do," he averred. He was short, dapper, dark-haired, and blue-eyed, with elegant manners. He loved the theatre and France, having first travelled to Paris in 1915, to report the war in pictures for *Puck*. Friends nicknamed him "the Commuter," for his frequent sojourns abroad. In 1927, the French government made him a chevalier of the Legion of Honor; the poet Paul Claudel, as French ambassador to the United States, presented the decoration. Also in 1927, *The New Yorker* ran a page and a half on Barton, under the title "Through the Magnifying Glass." The fact-crammed piece, by Charles G. Shaw, emphasizes the transatlantic dandy's clothes:

MIGUEL COVARRUBIAS
Ralph Barton, c. 1927

His haberdashery comes from Charvet's, Place Vendôme, and embraces a varied assortment of colored striped shirts, with drawers and collars of the same material to match each shirt, white silk undershirts, beige silk pajamas (emblazoned with white frogs), and white, watered-silk suspenders. Each of his pairs of trousers has its own pair of suspenders. . . . In Paris he carries a walking stick; in New York a sword cane. . . . In lieu of a scarfpin, a scarab seal ring encircles his cravat, and when indoors he is partial to Chinese slippers. . . . Chanel No. 22 is his customary perfume. His favored dressing gown is of a gallant jade hue.

Barton's highly specific tastes in champagne, wine, cigarettes, drawing pen, paper, and ink are also confided. We learn that he is remarkably tidy in person and, in his work, rapid but tardy; and we are told that he loathes mathematics, cannot drive, is sick of jazz, "rarely touches gin or whiskey but is extremely fond of Château Yquem," and "has been in love ninety-two times in all." What's more, he has never voted, served on a jury, or contributed to charity. Though "in temperament he is definitely Latin," this exquisite "creature of the cosmopolis" may be one-sixteenth Cherokee, if we can credit "a scandalous legend to the effect that his great-great-grandmother was a beautiful Cherokee maid."

When Harold Ross founded *The New Yorker* in 1925, Barton figured as an advisory editor, a stockholder, and a prominent contributor, providing not only theatrical caricatures but tart and droll short reviews as captions. But Barton's frequent long stays in France interrupted the flow of his contributions. Surprisingly, he did only one cover for the magazine—a cartoon of angry Christmas shoppers. Ross, a man of many nervous reactions, was made uneasy by what he felt was a macabre streak in Barton's work, and Barton, though a personal friend, was not his favorite artist—Peter Arno was—nor anything like as central to the young magazine's workings and look as Rea Irvin. Ross preferred to sponsor fresh talents rather than further reputations already established, and in the mid-Twenties Barton was riding high. In addition to doing copious magazine work, he designed and painted (from a scaffold!) a theatre curtain—a panorama of caricatures—for the revue *Chauve-Souris,* and saw another panoramic drawing of celebrities made into an Americana dress print. In 1925 he illustrated Anita Loos's best-selling novel *Gentlemen Prefer Blondes* and in 1928 its sequel, *But Gentlemen Marry Brunettes.*

Barton married four times, and fathered two daughters—Natalie by the first wife, née Marie Jennings, and by his second wife, Anne Minnerly (who next married E. E. Cummings), a second daughter, Diana. His third wife, the actress Carlotta Monterey, became Eugene O'Neill's third wife, and Barton's fourth wife, Germaine Tailleferre, was a well-known French composer—a member, with Poulenc and Milhaud, of Les Six.

One month after his fourth divorce was final, and a few days after Carlotta had returned from Europe with O'Neill, Barton committed suicide, three months short of his fortieth birthday. Around midnight on May 19, 1931, in his penthouse apartment at 419 East Fifty-seventh Street, he typed out a long note which he titled "OBIT" in red ink; placed it and a shorter note to the maid on a table; laid on his bed a copy of Gray's *Anatomy* open to an illustration of the human heart; got into bed in silk pajamas; pulled the covers up to his chin; and, while holding a cigarette in his left hand, shot himself through the right temple.

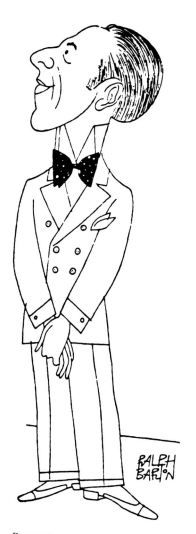

BARTON
Self-caricature, c. 1925

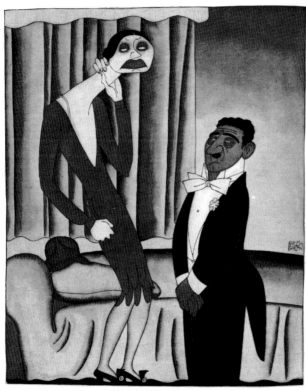

"THE GREEN HAT"
Miss Cornell's Latest and Mr. Arlen's First Triumph in the Theatre

THE talented Miss Katherine Cornell, the *Iris March* of the stage version of "The Green Hat," and Mr. Michael Arlen (*né* Kouyoumdjian), its author, stop to consider things between acts.

At latest reports, the line at the box office reached from the Broadhurst Theatre to the Battery, with Miss Gertrude Ederle treading water in the Bay. Mr. Arlen is thus repeating the magnificent clean-up that he made in Chicago and Detroit. "The Green Hat" is full of the most delicious pathological and obstetrical conversation for those who never have any fun at home.—R. B.

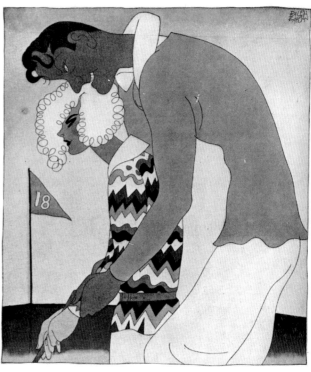

BIRDIES OR BETTER
Mr. A. H. Woods Has Openers for the 1925-26 Season

BEGINNING next week copies of Spaulding's Golf Guide and Rules of Golf, as approved by the Royal and Ancient Golf Club of St. Andrews and adopted by the United States Golf Association, will be on sale in the lobby of Maxine Elliott's Theatre. You can not understand "Spring Fever," the new Vincent Lawrence comedy, without the Golf Guide. Names of the players, their handicaps and a score card will be presented, gratis, with the program.

In the vista *supra*, the blonde and lovely Miss Marion Coakley is receiving instructions in how to smite the ball for a drive into the second balcony by the excellent Mr. James Rennie, who plays a handsome roughneck. This is in the first act. In the third act, Mr. Rennie receives instructions from Miss Coakley in that art and pastime in which the ladies always excel, and which needs no Guide to be perfectly clear to the veriest novice.—R. B.

BARTON
Cartoons from
The New Yorker, 1925

His death was front-page news in *The New York Times* of May 21st. The headline RALPH BARTON ENDS / HIS LIFE WITH PISTOL got equal billing with CIVIL WAR IN CHINA / IS STARTING NORTH. The *Times* told how his maid, Mary Jefferson, had observed his black mood when he returned to the apartment on May 19th. She said to him, "You're not going to do anything foolish? If you are, I'm going to stay here." The story continues, "The artist laughed and said it was safe for her to go." She found his body when she came back to the penthouse around ten the next morning; the note to her accompanied thirty-five dollars as pay and apologized for its not being more. A curious crowd gathered outside the apartment building, but only his brother, Homer, a New York actor, and, in the afternoon, the artist Neysa McMein were admitted. Homer said to reporters, "It was a matter of impulse, I am sure, for Ralph was very impulsive. . . . Ralph did not consider his action, I know, because he was looking forward to the summer in the apartment. He had brought in some new flower boxes to decorate it." Barton's redoubtable mother, reached in Kansas City, said, "I can't believe Ralph shot himself. There must be something about that we do not know." His sister, Ethel (Mrs. Louis J. Klein), said, "Ralph was such a gentle spirited person that it seems impossible that he should have had a gun in his apartment."

The assistant medical examiner, Raymond B. Miles, took the open Gray's *Anatomy* to indicate that Barton had contemplated shooting himself through the heart, and had decided against it. The police released the text of the "OBIT" that Barton had composed, and the *Times* reproduced it in full, singling out for sensationalistic emphasis its pathetic homage to the present Mrs. O'Neill, "my beautiful lost angel, Carlotta, the only woman I ever loved and whom I respect and admire above all the rest of the human race. She is the one person who could have saved me had I been savable. She did her best. No one ever had a more devoted or more understanding wife. I do hope that she will understand what my malady was and forgive me a little." His note concluded, "I kiss my dear children—and Carlotta," and was signed not with his name but with seven "X"s.

The "dear children"—his two daughters—scarcely figure in the skimpy Barton literature. In the newspaper stories following his death, a paragraph from the Kansas City *Times* (the *Star*'s morning version) of May 21, 1931, tells, with several misstatements of fact, how Barton and Chaplin, during the English trip earlier that year, had visited Natalie at a convent in Hackney. The twenty-year-old novice "could speak to them, shyly and only for a moment, from the cloistered precincts." The story goes on:

> Another daughter, Diana, 10, is in school in Lausanne, Switzerland. Today after Barton had been found dead, a letter came addressed to him in childish handwriting. On the envelope was a heart, with an arrow, and the legend, "I love you." That was from Diana.

In fact, Diana, born on June 20, 1921, was then a month shy of ten. Natalie had been born on October 1, 1910, eleven months after her parents had married at the juvenile ages of eighteen and fifteen. A somewhat

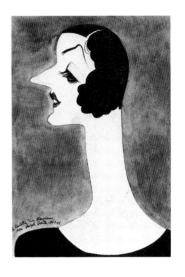

BARTON
Portrait of Carlotta Monterey
Watercolor, pencil, and enamel
paint, 10 1/2 × 14 3/4"
Collection of Mrs. Nickolas
Muray, New York

florid serial biography in *College Humor* early in 1932, by Dorothy Giles, states that Barton, when he was divorcing his first wife in 1917 (he sued, she apparently having found comfort with a Kansas City *Star* artist, Herbert Grout, during Barton's first French excursion), was awarded custody of Natalie. For a time he and the little girl lived together in an apartment in Washington Heights. A friend is quoted as saying, "I don't believe he was ever as truly happy again as he was just then, when he and Natalie were together." However, when he and his second wife divorced in 1922, Barton went to Paris and Natalie was placed in a Kansas City convent school, run by the Sisters of Notre Dame de Sion. In 1929, his "dark-eyed, beautiful" daughter announced her decision to become a nun, and he took her off with him to tour Europe for a year. Dorothy Giles writes:

> He would show her the world and its glories, then let her decide[,] if she would, to give it up.
>
> But at the year's end, with Italy behind them, with London and Paris and Vienna offering their all, her answer was the same—
>
> "I want to be a nun."
>
> And true to his own agnostic's code of allowing to each mind freedom to decide its own fate, he agreed. With a sardonic smile he drew the check for his daughter's dowry, in her cloister.

The author then asks, "I wonder if that isn't really the end of Ralph Barton's story?"

Barton and Carlotta, a former Miss California, shared a bed from 1923 to 1926—the third marriage for both. They were renowned for their parties. Barbara and Arthur Gelb's biography of Eugene O'Neill quotes the photographer Nickolas Muray: "Ralph and Carlotta used to give very lavish parties. I remember one party when Jimmy Walker was present. Another time they had a professional wrestling match staged in their living room. And at one party Charlie Chaplin, who was an intimate friend of Ralph's . . . arrived and took over. He did double-talk in half a dozen languages. . . . He played a number of instruments—violin, trombone, clarinet, piano, among others. There was an apparently inexhaustible supply of food and liquor, always elegantly served." And Ilka Chase recalled, "I used to love to go there, because they had wonderful books and pictures and delicious little dinners; but they dined at half past six even when Carlotta wasn't playing, and I never could understand why. It had something to do with their temperaments, I imagine; their temperaments were

BARTON
Cartoon from
The New Yorker, 1930

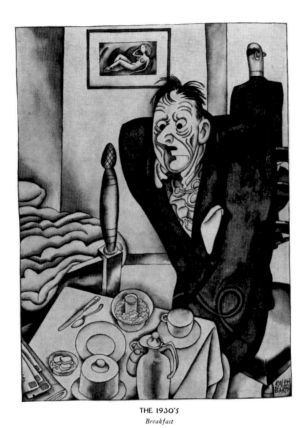

THE 1930'S
Breakfast

prominent, and everybody relaxed when they got a divorce." In their divorce action, Carlotta charged Barton, an incorrigible philanderer, with "misconduct at the Hotel des Artistes, 1 West Sixty-seventh Street."

His posthumous homage was a considerable embarrassment to the O'Neills and may have been meant to be. Carl Van Vechten lunched with them on May 20th and later told an interviewer, "[Carlotta] couldn't understand why he'd dragged her into it. Barton, she insisted, hadn't loved her in years." In a statement to the press, she claimed that she had not seen or heard from her ex-husband "since her divorce from him more than five years ago." Van Vechten's reminiscence elaborates: "Personally, I thought it a clear case of ego, of his wanting all possible attention at his death. He resented her marrying someone more famous than himself and wanted to upset them. I knew Ralph intimately, I'd seen him only a short time before. He was heavily in debt, he'd lived beyond his means for years, he'd seen and done everything, and saw no point in going on. Don't forget, too, that the Great Depression was on—people weren't in the mood for his sophisticated art. The market for his stuff had shrunk, and he could see only lean times ahead, so he decided to go out in a splash of publicity."

The times, however, couldn't have been impossibly lean for an artist enjoying the friendship and patronage of Harold Ross, whose *New Yorker* was prospering amid the slump. Ross in a letter to Barton in France urged him to return: "You have got to conform to a certain extent and you had better do it here, regaining your old supremacy. Here you will be supreme again." Barton sometimes appeared twice in a single issue, and had created several running departments for himself—"The Inquiring Reporter," "Heroes of the Week," "The Graphic Section." The *New Yorker* scrapbooks show a flurry of Barton contributions in the weeks before his death, including a "Graphic Section" containing a small prophetic cameo of a man beyond cheering up. In addition to the heralded arrival of the

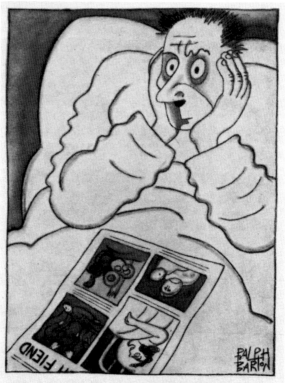

BARTON
From *The Graphic Section,*
in *The New Yorker,* 1931

THE MAN WHO STARTED THE DAY by reading a
tabloid newspaper contemplates the beauties of life.

O'Neills, Barton had recently been bothered by reports of his having been jilted by the five-and-dime heiress Ruth Kresge; the day after the O'Neills docked, she embarked for Europe with her fiancé, "Rufus Clark Caulkins, one-time Princeton football player." And, undoubtedly, Barton, who less than two years earlier had protested in an interview, "I have too much money," lost heavily in the stock-market crash. But his "OBIT" attempted a psychological self-diagnosis, blaming depression rather than the Depression:

> Any sane doctor knows that the reasons for suicide are invariably psychopathological and the true suicide type manufactures his own difficulties. I have had few real difficulties. I have had, on the contrary, an exceptionally glamorous life, as life goes; and I have had more than my share of affection and appreciation.
>
> The most charming, intelligent and important people I have known have liked me, and the list of my enemies is very flattering to me. I have always had excellent health, but since my early childhood I have suffered from a melancholia, which in the last five years has begun to show definite symptoms of manic-depressive insanity.
>
> It has prevented my getting anything like the full value out of my talent, and the past three years has made work a torture to do at all. It has made it impossible for me to enjoy the simple pleasures of life. I have run from wife to wife, from house to house and from country to country in a ridiculous effort to escape from myself. . . .
>
> No one thing is responsible for this and no one person—except myself. If the gossips insist on something more definite and thrilling as a reason, let them choose my pending appointment with the dentist or the fact that I happened to be painfully short of cash at the moment. . . . After all, one has to choose a moment; and the air is always full of reasons at any given moment. I did it because I am fed up with inventing devices for getting through twenty-four hours a day and with bridging over a few months periodically with some beautiful interest, such as a new gal who annoyed me to the point where I forgot my own troubles.

A man within minutes of ending his life must be listened to; Barton knew his own mental state. This was not his first suicide attempt. According to the United Press, Harold Ross, after Barton's death, revealed that eight months earlier the artist had poisoned himself and been narrowly revived by friends who found him in his apartment. Two months after this, he accompanied Neysa McMein to Charleston, where he bought a revolver. His tendency toward depression had been noticed by many

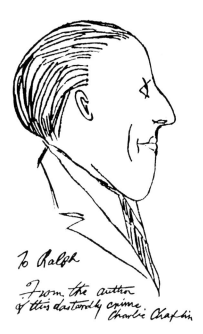

To Ralph

*From the author
of this dastardly crime.
Charlie Chaplin*

CHARLIE CHAPLIN
Ralph Barton, 1931

friends, including Chaplin, who earlier in 1931, because of Barton's low spirits, had invited him at the last minute to join a jaunt to the London premiere of *City Lights*. Barton's behavior in London became pathological. According to David Robinson's biography of Chaplin, "After the first week or so, [Barton] could not be persuaded to leave the Carlton Hotel, but wandered the suite and the public corridors." He was seen fondling the revolver, and on one occasion "Chaplin was alarmed and irritated to discover that Barton had cut the wires on the electric clocks, for reasons known only to himself." Chaplin paid for his return passage and gave him twenty-five pounds, since Barton appeared to be penniless. Somewhere in their time together those last months, Chaplin sketched a caricature of Barton; it has a sad redolence absent from Miguel Covarrubias's caricature, and Barton's own, both of which emphasize the dandy. Barton's more painterly self-portrait of around 1922, however, is deeply melancholic. Its elongated face reminded him of El Greco, and he inscribed it "With apologies to Greco / and God / RB."

His childhood was saturated in religion, of an odd sort. In *The Jazz Age, as Seen Through the Eyes of Ralph Barton, Miguel Covarrubias, and John Held, Jr.,* the catalogue of a show of drawings put on at the museum of the Rhode Island School of Design in 1968, Richard Merkin, the organizer, writes of Barton, "From childhood he was on intimate terms with tragedy and with the mechanics of madness. His parents, heartbroken after the death of his young sister, became 'natural scientists,' and began their own religion. They published a small magazine and took in patients to be treated. It is certain that this had its effect on young Barton who quickly came to abhor the trappings of sickness and disease." Kansas City was the milieu of which Hemingway, in the story "God Rest You Merry, Gentlemen" (about a religious young man's self-mutilation), wrote, "The dirt blew off the hills that now have been cut down, and Kansas City was very like Constantinople." The Midwest had a sere spirituality that no amount of acquired atheism and Eastern sophistication could quench. Apologies to God kept coming. Barton's was an extreme case of what Merkin calls "the exaggerated urbanity of the provincial." Even New York wasn't urbane enough for him, and in Paris, in the words of Thomas Craven, "he out-fopped the French at their own game, dressed like something midway between a toreador and an aesthete, and had many imitators among the young caricaturists." Socially, Barton had chosen to make a splash and to run with the rich and the very famous, which

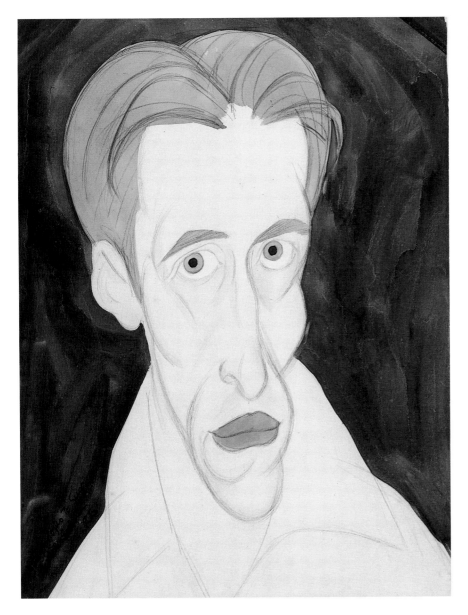

BARTON
Self-portrait, c. 1922
Watercolor and pencil,
14 3/4 × 11″
National Portrait Gallery,
Smithsonian Institution,
Washington, D.C.

is a hard race for a working artist to maintain. Yet the facility, confidence, and fineness of his work right to the end lead us to decry his suicide, and to scan this work's lighthearted surface for a clue.

His drawings, like Modigliani's, combine a high pitch of sensuality with a passion for design. The two artists shared a taste for the archaic: Barton

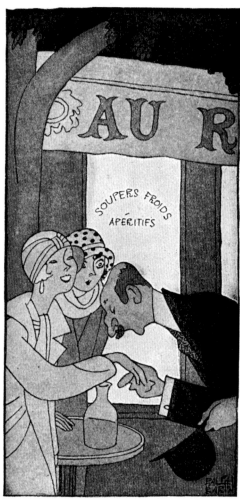

"*Kissing your hand may make you feel very good but a diamond bracelet lasts forever.*"

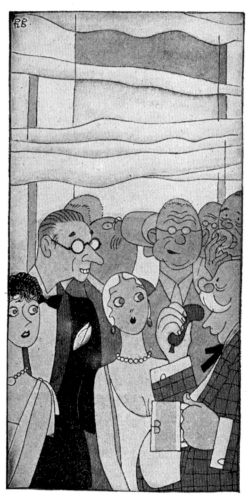

"*The Germans stand in the lobby of the theatre and eat quite a lot of Bermudian onions and garlick sausage.*"

(Above and opposite)
BARTON   Illustrations from *Gentlemen Prefer Blondes* (Boni & Liveright, 1925)

once claimed, "The old Greeks taught me. . . . I used to go up to the Metropolitan Museum and spend hours studying the figures and decorations on ancient Greek pottery." He liked a tight space. His little illustrations for *Gentlemen Prefer Blondes* are fitted into narrow, tall rectangles, crammed with truncated detail like lucid keyholes. Where the top of a panel threatens to be empty, as in the picture of "Dr. Froyd," the artist fills it with satisfyingly animated scallops and fringe buttons. The illustrations for the Boni and Liveright limited edition of Balzac's *Droll Stories*, however, constitute his masterpiece in this line. Executed during Barton's marriage to Germaine Tailleferre, they consummate his lifelong Francophilia; he travelled to Touraine for appropriate architectural detail, which overflows the backgrounds. The foregrounds are, thanks to the nature of the tales, more often than not occupied by naked females, and these enchanting nudes in sum sing Barton's hymn to life. The men in the illustrations are often cuckolded or impotent, alienated from vitality and beauty; in one scene of marital discontent the artist has troubled to carve the bedpost with a full depiction of that primal estrangement, the Fall and Expulsion from Eden. In another connubial scene, the behorned husband seems to bay at the moon while bedclothes and bed-curtains are possessed by a rhythmic agitation of restlessness and longing. The sleeping woman with her bared breast is alone tranquil; the visual repository of purity, she is exempt from what Max Jacob, in speaking of Modigliani, called "a need for crystalline purity." Such a need can easily encourage self-destructiveness—for what is purer than death?

Of Modigliani Jacob also said that he was "cutting, but as fragile as glass." The *Times* obituary, presumably voicing the contemporary verdict, spoke of Barton's "cynical style of art" and of "a devastating humor and a bitter irony," and stated, "His writings were like his drawings—sharp." Yet Barton's drawings, these many decades later, do not seem especially cutting. His generalized cartoon figures have something of the lollipop-headed innocence of his contemporary John Held, Jr.,'s sheiks and flappers. Barton's caricatures

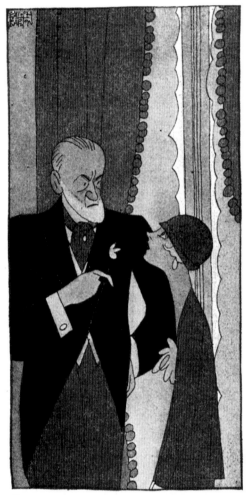

"Dr. Froyd seemed to think that I was quite a famous case."

(Overleaf) BARTON
Illustrations for *Droll Stories*,
by Honoré de Balzac,
limited edition in two volumes
(Boni & Liveright, 1928)

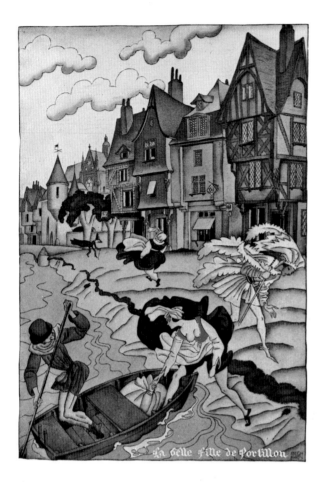

La belle fille de Portillon

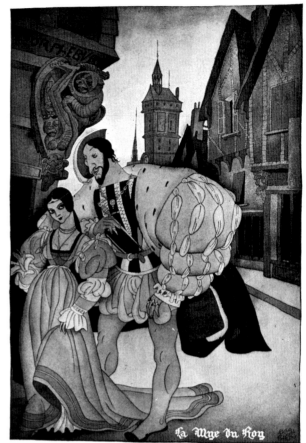

La Mye du Roy

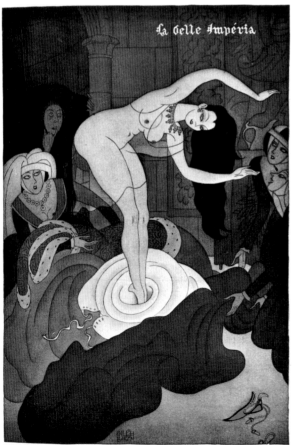

La belle Impéria

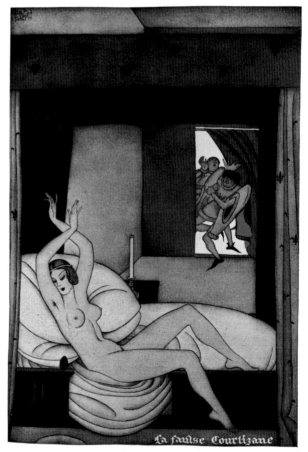

La faulse Courtizane

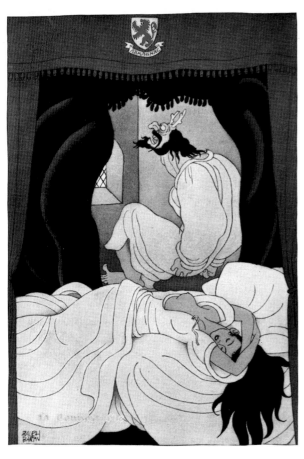

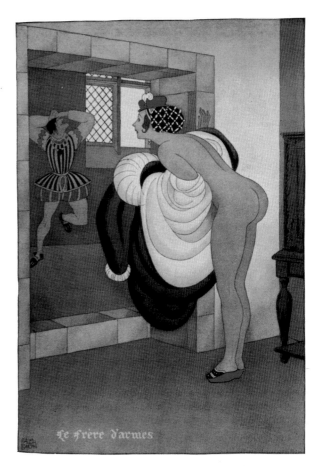

Le frère d'armes

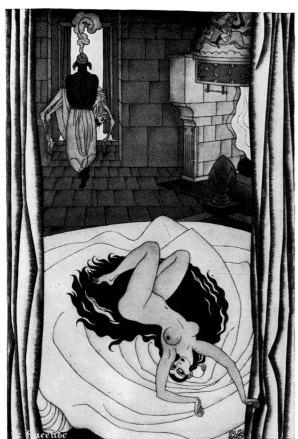

Succube

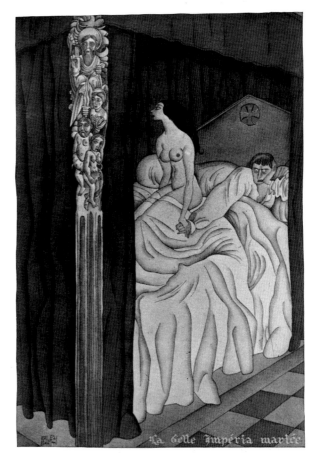

La belle Impéria mariée

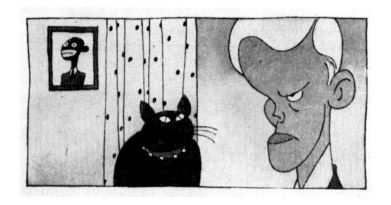

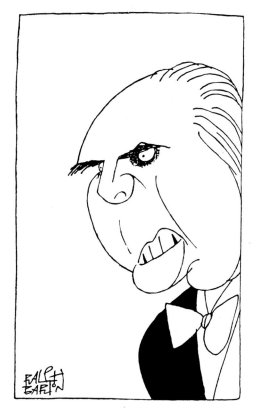

BARTON
(Above) *Carl Van Vechten* from *The Inquiring Reporter*,
in *The New Yorker*, 1925

(Right) *Theodore Dreiser* from *Heroes of the Week*,
in *The New Yorker*, 1926

are not indignant, like Daumier's, or frenzied, like Gerald Scarfe's; they
are decoratively descriptive. In reviewing a book by Covarrubias, Barton
wrote, "It is not the caricaturist's business to be penetrating; it is his job
to put down the figure a man cuts before his fellows in his attempt to
conceal the writhings of his soul." He had the born caricaturist's abnor-
mal sensitivity to facial configuration, and a casual expertise at tellingly
finding his way among the interlocking bumps and creases of physiog-
nomy. Dreiser's dishevelled snarl and Van Vechten's complacent jut of
lip are reduced to the linear minimum as dispassionately as the mummi-
fied images of Calhoun and Clay. Barton admired Max Beerbohm, and,
though the Englishman's line is as woolly and limp as the American's is
wiry and crisp, an affinity can be felt in the carefree anatomy and formal
balance of their tableaux.

But the dry, donnish inscriptions on Beerbohm's drawings were beyond
Barton, or beyond the audience available to him, and the dandy from

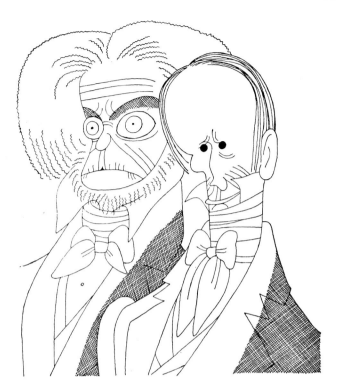

*John C. Calhoun and Henry Clay, co-authors and
producers of, though not actors in, the war of 1812.*

Kansas City produced no equivalent of the small but exquisite body of
essays and parodies that give Max a permanent niche in English literature.
Among the non-chemical reasons for Barton's growing unhappiness must
have been the failure of his career to develop a significant literary side,
though he sporadically exerted himself in that direction. "He sticks out
his tongue while working and would rather write than draw," Charles G.
Shaw declared. Barton wrote two books. His *Science in Rhyme Without
Reason* (1924) is a spirited exercise in the light-verse mode then fashionable, slight but delightfully illustrated, and showing—perhaps not surprisingly in a man whose father wrote of the "twenty-six basic lessons in
the science of life"—a certain systematical turn of mind: the book has a
bibliography and an index, and its contents tackle, in alphabetical order,
"Aeronautics," "Æsthetics," "Astronomy," "Bacteriology," etc. As a
poet, Barton can be hasty and metrically unstrict but also deft. The dedi-
cation runs, touchingly in light of later events:

Please accept these *entremets,*
Sweet Carlotta Monterey.

"Evolution" lays out with considerable precision such prehistorical developments as

A hydrosphere then did appear,
Which fell to earth as boiling tears,
And, after several million years,
Produced some rather tepid seas

and

In order came the zoophyte;
The Palæolithic trilobite;
True fishes, crabs amphibian;
Then reptiles in the Permian;
And then the giant dinosaurs,
And next our flying ancestors.

"Natural History," but for its awkward fourth line, is a perfect little verbal mechanism:

The Cuckoo
Is at its best
In clocks.
Outside of clocks
It stocks
The titlark's nest
With eggs;
Then begs
Both food and rest.
It thrives;
But drives
The titlark coo-coo.

Though no Hilaire Belloc or Arthur Guiterman, Barton plays their game acceptably, somewhat as Chaplin could play the clarinet, the violin, the trombone, and the piano. Barton's one prose volume, *God's Country* (1929), constitutes a less happy attempt to turn systematic exposition into jokes—a 330-page facetious revisionist history of the United States from Columbus to Hoover. The Presidents are lampooned as monarchs (Zachary the Rough and Ready, Franklin the Debonair); the Presidency is

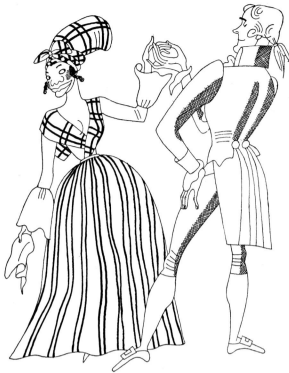

Thomas I stepping a measure with Deborah, his favorite slave.

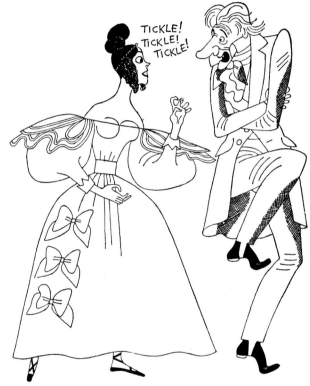

TICKLE!
TICKLE!
TICKLE!

Pretty Peggy O'Neal and Andrew I, called "Old Hickory."

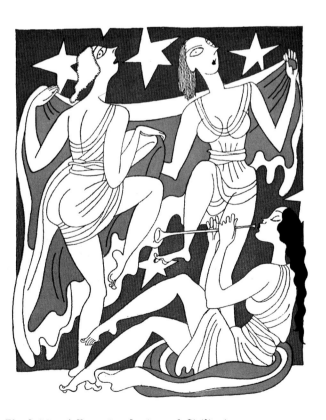

The Spirits of Humanity, Justice and Civilization as interpreted by junior members of the Women's League of Women for the benefit of the Women's Memorial Fund.

BARTON
Illustrations from
God's Country (1929)

renamed the Misterhood; fanciful contending parties such as Uniboodlists and Multiboodlists (an echo of the Unity School of Christianity and its Trinitarian competitors?) are invented; and sexual shenanigans not entirely fanciful are numbered among the Presidential acts. Barton had done his homework, and some bleak historical truths register: "They [the American people] elected Franklin Pierce to the Misterhood because they felt that his absolutely colorless record gave promise that he would not annoy them with the political issues of the day." Ring Lardner's flights into nonsense, H. L. Mencken's mockery of the American booboisie and its sacred myths, and a fashionable left-wing scorn of capitalism stand behind *God's Country;* but the flippant, bantering tone suitable to capsule theatre notices does not quite do when it is applied to the grave facts of history. Here, for instance, is Barton's verbal cartoon of Lincoln's assassination:

> On the evening of the 14th of April, 1865, Abraham attended Ford's Theatre in Washington. When he entered his box, a great burst of applause went up from the house, for the people of his time loved and appreciated him. The Mister was obliged to stand up and take bow after bow. An actor out of work, standing at the back of the house, became blind with jealousy at the sight of a non-Equity man getting such a hand. He entered the box from the rear and shot Abraham dead.
>
> Dead, that is, as far as this mortal coil is concerned. On the morrow, God sent a shaft of pure white light down from on high to Number 576 Tenth

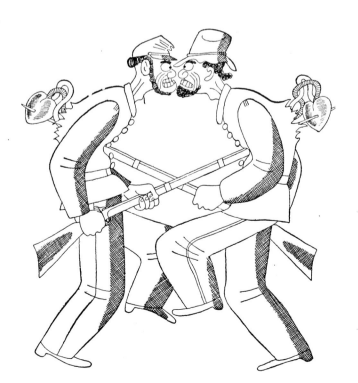

BARTON
From *God's Country* (1929)

Street, N. W., and sucked his immortal soul up to the Public Thing of heaven. There, Abraham joined the company of the saints, for there is nothing that the Almighty admires so much as a man who has served as Mister of the United States during a bloody war.

It makes a queer mix: the date and the address are exact, the assassination's motivation is farcical, and the Almighty's alleged fondness for bloody Presidents needs to be more earnestly examined. As in the Civil War sketch that accompanies this chapter, real hearts (thanks, perhaps, to Gray's *Anatomy*) pop disturbingly from papery bodies. A real indignation ineffectively seethes within Barton's burlesque of American history; a kind of prolonged sneer results, that too rarely provokes either outright laughter or serious thought. "Repellent," "not much fun," "rather dull," and "entirely negligible" were among the epithets of contemporary reviewers. *God's Country,* published in the year of the stock-market crash, flopped, and Barton never again tried anything so ambitious. His years of not "getting anything like the full value out of my talent" had begun. Yet what a talent it was! Even hobbled by melancholy and spendthrift ways, it outclassed most of the competition. The *Times,* the day after it reported the suicide, groped to express a sense of loss, adding this to an account of a press conference that O'Neill gave: "In the meanwhile the body of the artist . . . lay in lonely state in one of the small chapels of the Campbell Funeral Church. The city which had once acclaimed his work had apparently forgotten him."

We do not expect our humorous artists to die young. Tenniel and Shepard drew and sold into their nineties; George Price and William Steig, who first appeared in *The New Yorker* during Ralph Barton's last year, are still hard at it, week after week. Barton's chucked career hauntingly reverberates. Neysa McMein, herself a dedicated professional, asked him while they were in Charleston together, "Don't you want to be a great artist? Of course, you are a swell artist now, but don't you want a great future?" He answered, "No, I think not. I've had everything." A few days later, he bought himself a pistol, having failed to do the job with poison. Six months later, he used it. With his final debonair gesture, the creator of the black-hearted ashman appropriated for himself the Stygian glamour of those poets who, despairing of the noise, opt for silence.

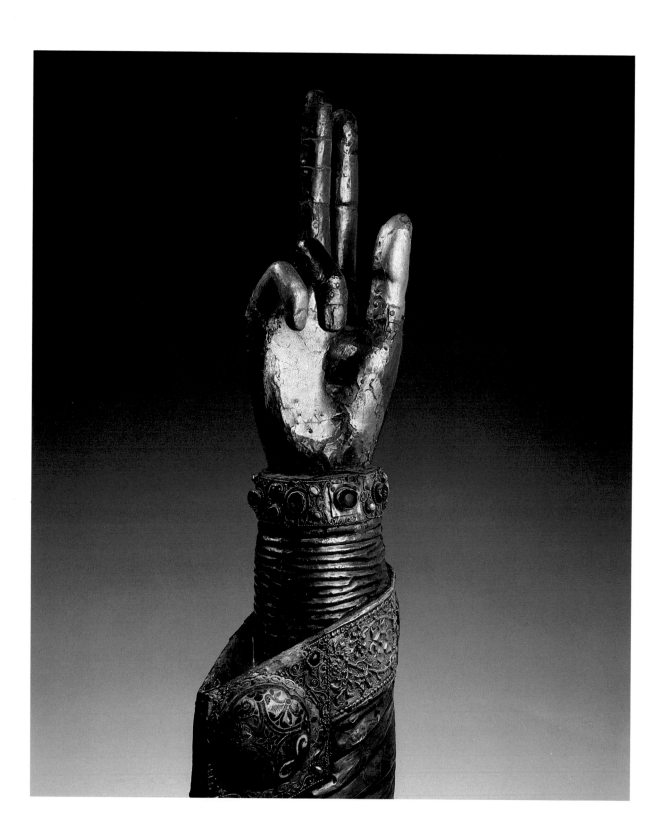

The Hand of Saint Saens

———

THE HUMAN HAND is a miraculous thing. Without its opposable thumb, we are told, we'd all still be monkeys, chattering away on the gloomy far side of fire, tools, Euclid, cathedrals, and chess by mail. Edmund Wilson, holding a book in his hand in 1936, "suddenly saw it as an animal's paw with the fingers lengthened to claws and become prehensile for climbing around." Actually, hands came before paws. The primitive amphibian *Labyrinthodont* crawled up on the shore three hundred or so million years ago with five digits fore and aft just like you and me. Many of the two-legged dinosaurs, from little *Compsognathus* to mighty *Tyrannosaurus,* had dainty forearms tipped with hands not so different from ours and, like ours, used for holding prey. Except among primates, the evolutionary trend in mammals has been away from the archaic heritage of five elongated digits toward the simplifications of paws and hooves and elephant feet. Man, in his extremities, remains relatively little evolved, but for the thumb's crucial adaptation.

Our hands are among the first parts of ourselves we notice. They remain toys, even when we stop sucking on them. They can be made to walk on two fingers and to enact mock combats and comic routines on the stage of a desktop or counterpane. Pink headless homunculi, they represent the whole man, lifted skyward in petition or clasped in the hand of another in comradeship. They take upon themselves a universal dualism,

Artist unknown
The Hand of Saint Saens
(*Bras Reliquaire de Saint Saens*),
12th century
Wooden core covered with gold, hammered silver, and enameled medallions
Musée Départemental des Antiquités, Rouen

the one being *right* and (in many traditions) clean, the other being sinister and gauche and unclean. If we draw, our free hand is the first piece of our anatomy that can be (handily) studied and that will patiently pose. No wonder the history of drawing is full of superbly rendered hands—Leonardo's the loveliest, Michelangelo's the most deeply articulated and dynamic, Dürer's famous praying hands a little sickly and perhaps fittingly turned into a pious cliché.

The hand here is lifted in blessing. Its stylized form once contained real bone, for it is a wooden reliquary fashioned to hold the arm of Saint Saens, an Irish-French saint of a sublime obscurity. A reliquary enwraps the withered, desiccated, invisible actual within an aesthetic creation. We feel slightly squeamish, as whenever the boundary between art and reality is unsteady—for other instance, Fabergé eggs, trompe l'œil paintings, and George Segal sculptures.

In a reliquary, form and content have a relationship that inverts that of traditional sculpture, whose content is brute stone or wood or metal, and whose form bestows meaning and life. Here, it was the dead saint who gave matter meaning, by so forcefully dedicating his body to the mysteries of the Spirit that holiness still clings to his corpse and generates miracles. The reliquarist merely fabricates a shell whose durability symbolizes eternity. Yet with what elegance this anonymous craftsman has shaped his case!—a bejewelled piece of Gothic thrust, stiff as a spire, yet with something shapely in the bare hand that suggests the seductive, vinelike hands of Hindu sculpture. The riveted Band-Aids, testifying to damage repaired, enhance the dignity of the absent saint's benign and alert gesture. Jewel thieves, perhaps miraculously, have been warded off. And what a noble thumb!

The Vital Push

JEAN IPOUSTEGUY, born in Dun-sur-Meuse in 1920, may be France's foremost living sculptor, but he is little known in the United States. Two of his large bronze statues, *David et Goliath* and *Homme poussant la porte* (*Man Pushing the Door*), are on permanent display in the Sculpture Garden of the Hirshhorn Museum in Washington, and three marble pieces appeared in the Guggenheim's fiftieth-anniversary exhibition; but his thrusting name doesn't carry beyond professional art circles and his only one-man American show was held in 1964, at the Albert Loeb Gallery. Ipoustéguy's mature work is baroque and surreal and may strike Americans as excessively literary. He has a Frenchman's gift for delivering elegant aphorisms to interviewers; e.g., "*Tout est visage pour être dévisagé, puis envisagé de nouveau*" ("Everything is a visage, a countenance to be discountenanced, then envisaged anew") and "*Dieu créa la pesanteur pour se protéger des tuiles qui menacent le ciel*" ("God created weight to protect Himself against the stones that threaten the sky") and "*La sculpture n'est pas faite pour fonctionner, mais pour nous faire fonctionner*" ("Sculpture is not made to function, but to make us function") and "*L'objet, tout comme la machine, est en plein sur les nombres; l'Anti-objet (l'œuvre-d'art) procède de l'intervalle entre les nombres*" ("The object, like the machine, is right on the numbers; the anti-object [the work of art] comes out of the *gap* between the numbers").

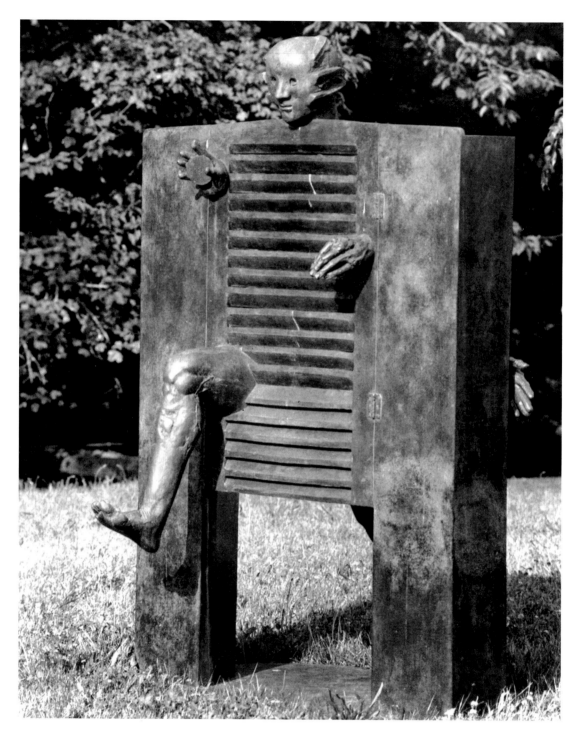

JEAN IPOUSTEGUY   *Homme poussant la porte* (front), 1966. Bronze, 78 × 57 × 46″
Hirshhorn Museum and Sculpture Garden, Smithsonian Institution, Washington, D.C.

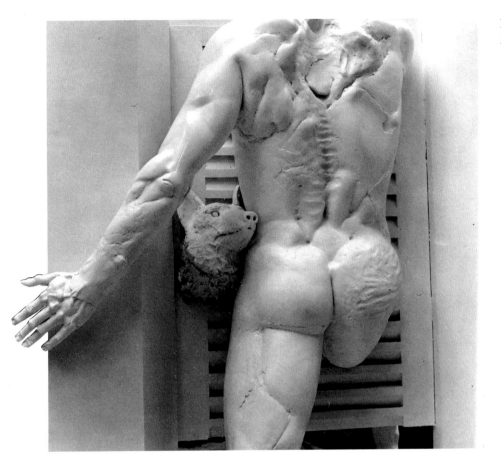

Homme poussant la porte (1966), perhaps his best-known work in this country (the Hirshhorn has made a postcard of it), seems from the front, with its round-eyed robotic head and its tensely uplifted foot poking through the unbudged louvered door, a mere joke; it is the figure's back, solemnly articulated and patchily rough and unexpectedly nuzzled by the head of a dog coming the other way, that reveals the sculptor's strange half-smiling power. *David et Goliath* (1959) offers a more typical example of the Ipoustéguy style—complex masses whose representational content is rather sinisterly subverted, and a bronze texture whose opaque mat smoothness—glossy but not burnished, like polished slate—is corroded as if by the action of acid or antiquity, with seams where the sculptor has apparently neglected to smooth together segments of carapace. David's helmeted head is thrown back as if to crow, but his face can be read

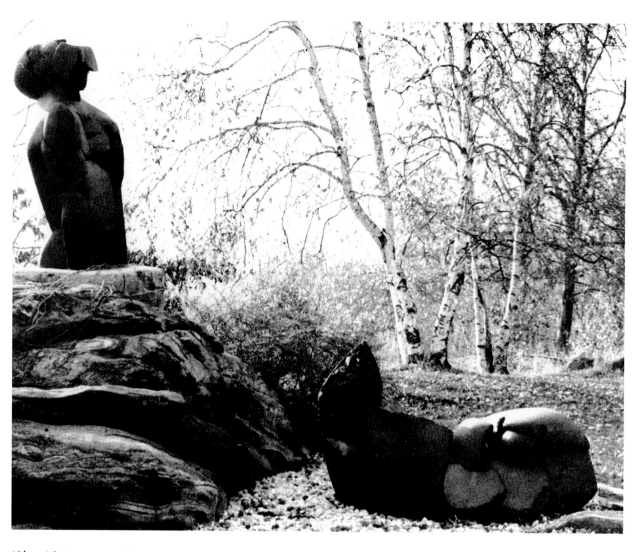

(Above) IPOUSTEGUY
David et Goliath, 1959
Bronze, 55 × 27 × 29″ (David),
59 × 27 × 29″ (Goliath)
Hirshhorn Museum and
Sculpture Garden, Smithsonian
Institution, Washington, D.C.

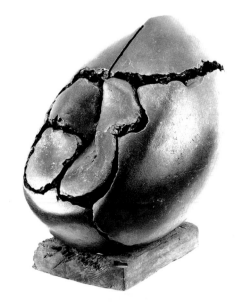

(Right) *Le Casque fendu,* 1958
Bronze, 14 × 11 ½ × 23″
Galerie Claude Bernard, Paris

no more easily than an insect's face. Decapitated Goliath (originally mounted at a considerably lower level, in a French setting of natural rock) has been reduced to an unintelligible jumble of shattered stone. The contrast of extreme finish and lack of finish is a traditional sculptor's flourish; but in certain works of Ipoustéguy it seems to bear witness less to the maker's hand than to the assaultive hand of decay or willful destruction. *Le Casque fendu* (*The Split Helmet*, 1958) immediately preceded *David et Goliath* and seems a study for it. Ipoustéguy has said of himself and his career, "*J'ai cassé l'œuf de Brancusi*" ("I broke Brancusi's egg"). The appearance of breakage, truncation, and fragmentation reminds us, too, of the mutilated and weathered masterpieces of sculpture that have descended to us from those long ages before the Renaissance generated its perfect simulacrums and modernism evolved the streamlined nuggets epitomized by Brancusi's work.

Ipoustéguy's œuvre also alludes to *écorché* anatomization, those horrifying yet illuminating drawings and models, loveliest and coolest in their French examples, that peel back the human body layer by layer. In *Petit écorché* and *Scène comique de la vie moderne* (both from 1976), the allusion is blunt, but frequently, as in the back and feet of *Homme poussant la porte*, anatomical details have a flayed, not fully fleshed look. Skin, absent or present, preoccupies Ipoustéguy as he considers the multiplicity of appearances: "*Nous possédons deux visages, celui qui* est à l'air *et celui qui* est au sang, *ce dernier calqué à l'intérieur de l'autre, sous l'épiderme*" ("We have two faces, one of which exists in the air and the other in the blood, the latter traced inside the other, under the skin"). His sculptures wear a variety of skins, from the marmoreal gloss of early, Brancusi-egg-breaking semi-abstractions like *La Rose* (1954) and *Le Crabe et l'oiseau*

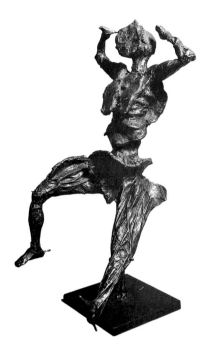

IPOUSTEGUY
Petit écorché, 1976
Bronze, 25 1/4 × 11 3/4 × 13 1/2″
Galerie Claude Bernard, Paris

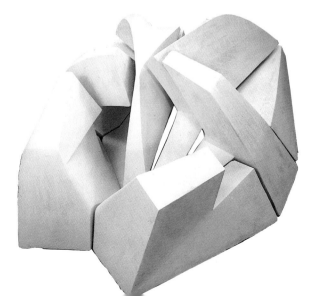

IPOUSTEGUY
La Rose, 1956
Marble, 37 × 46 × 46″
Galerie Claude Bernard, Paris

(Opposite and detail below)
IPOUSTEGUY
Femme au bain, 1966
Bronze, 59 × 78 3/4 × 43 3/4″
Galerie Claude Bernard, Paris

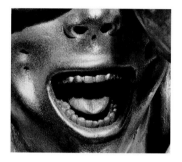

(1958) and the dazzlingly high polish of *La Naissance* (*The Birth*, 1968) and *La Femme au bain* (*Bathing Woman*, 1966) to textures of fracture, erosion, grainy cloth, crumbled clay, Giacomettiesque accumulated dribble, and squeezed and lumpy wax. His assemblage *Discours sous Mistra* (1964–66) appears to be a heap of weathered rocks; *Roger et le peuple des morts* (1961) embeds shells, nails, and cans in its crypt-slab; and the monumental *Alexandre avant Ecbatane* (1965) achieves a subtle porous roughness by having been carved in lightweight polystyrene, then cast from it as if by the lost-wax technique.

A thickset man ("*L'homme est trapu*," an interviewer has written) commonly photographed bare-chested at work, Ipoustéguy masters materials. Before moving to Choisy-le-Roi in 1949 and devoting himself pri-

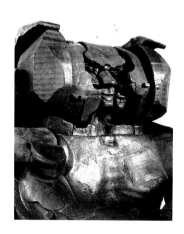

IPOUSTEGUY
Alexandre avant Ecbatane, 1965
Bronze, 67 × 39 1/2 × 79″
Galerie Claude Bernard, Paris

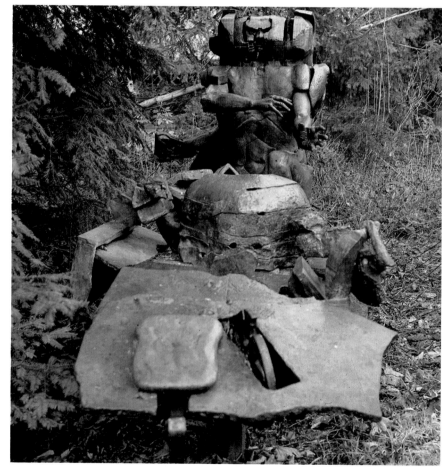

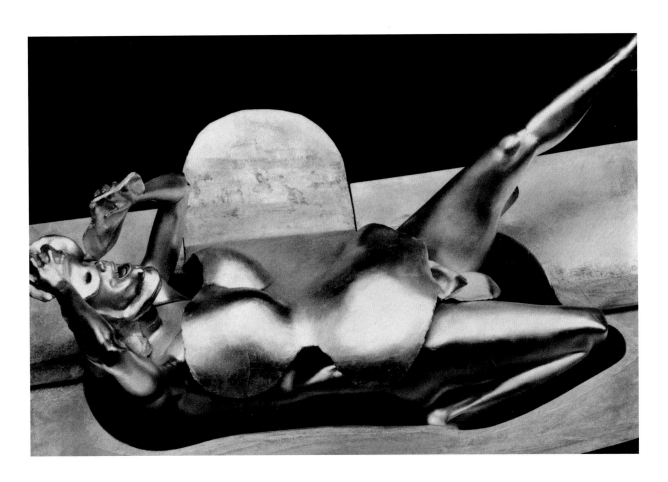

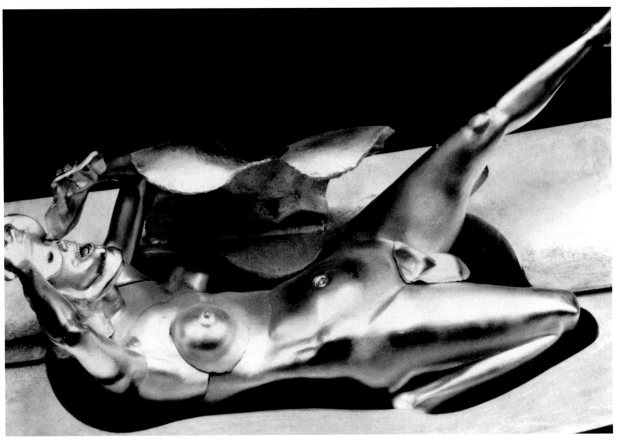

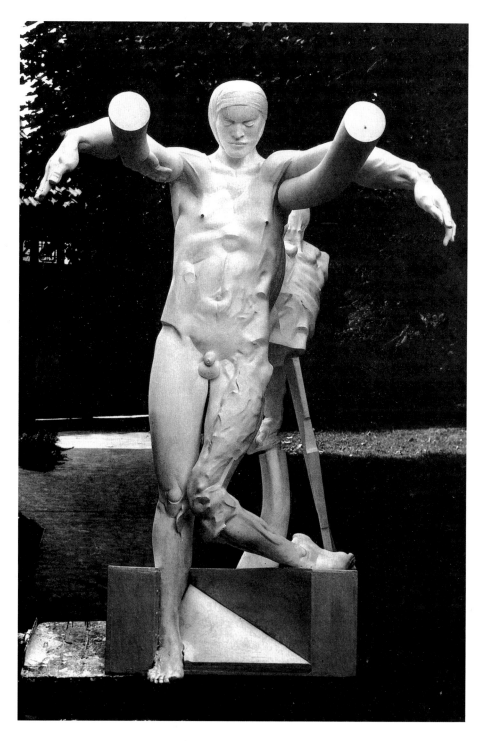

IPOUSTEGUY   *Val de Grâce*, 1977. Bronze, 86¹/₂ × 57 × 63″
Galerie Claude Bernard, Paris

marily to sculpture, he worked on and exhibited stained-glass windows, oil paintings, frescoes, lithographs, and tapestries. In the early Eighties he executed a series of chemically tinted bronzes of fruits and leaves (1982–84), and his recent large sculptures rather disagreeably mingle the human body with tubular forms and melt its muscular firmness into the weightless texture of paper (*Val de Grâce*, 1977; *A la lumière de chacun*, 1984). Committed to restoring sculpture to a pre-Brancusi complexity, Ipoustéguy draws upon virtuosic resources that remind us of the baroque masters, with their exuberant medleys of materials (metal, stone, colors of marble) and their ambitious assemblages of groups and entire environments. Unlike those many modern sculptors who are willing to work in materials as fragile as rope and clay and even sand, he employs only the least mutable of substances, disdaining even iron with its tendency to rust; for him, sculpture represents permanence: "*Le langage est fugace, la sculpture est permanence.*" This conviction consorts piquantly with his playfulness and his attempt to convey "*contradictions, vivantes contradictions.*" The sculptor creates works of permanence at the intersections of the inner and outer, the architectural and the human, the fluid and the frozen, the multiple and the single. "*Le sculpteur est celui qui a le don d'appréhender son élaboration de plusieurs points de l'espace à la fois et sa probité professionnelle l'oblige à localiser autour d'elle le plus grand nombre possible de lieux d'observation; j'y ajoute un poste supplémentaire situé au centre même de sa sculpture*" ("The sculptor is one who has the gift of apprehending the elaboration of many points in space at the same time, and his professional integrity obliges him to localize the greatest possible number of viewpoints; I add a supplementary standpoint situated at the very center of the sculpture"). The multiplicity of viewpoints helps account for the third hand in *Homme poussant la porte*, the third leg of *Homme* (1963), the three profiles and arms of *Alexandre*, and the several overlapping integuments of *Femme au bain*, including a secondary abdomen on hinges.

It accounts, too, for the two faces of the woman in *La Maison* (1976), executed in the more metallic, polished style Ipoustéguy has favored since his superb Sixties variations on classic stone sculpture—*Alexandre avant Ecbatane*, *Homme*, and *La Terre* (1963). *La Maison* emphasizes its metallic nature in the back view that reveals the male torso to be assembled of thick plates enclosing a geometric oval and a pelvis whose stylization is interrupted only by the half-emerged organic form of testicles. The male

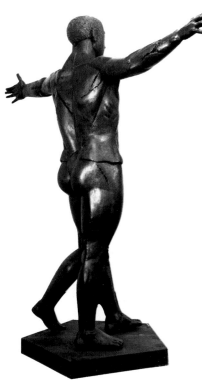

IPOUSTEGUY
Homme, 1963
Bronze, 79 × 82″
Galerie Claude Bernard, Paris

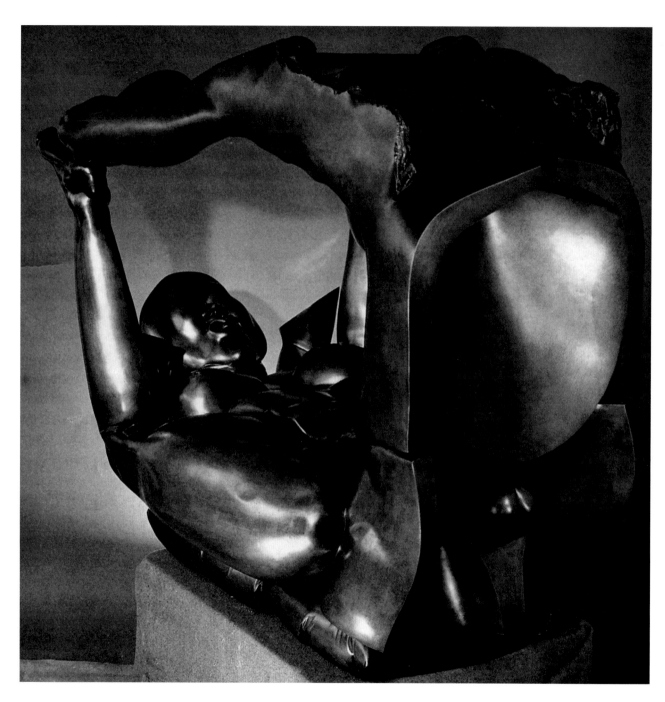

IPOUSTEGUY   *La Maison* (back), 1976. Bronze, 55 × 39 × 50″
Galerie Claude Bernard, Paris

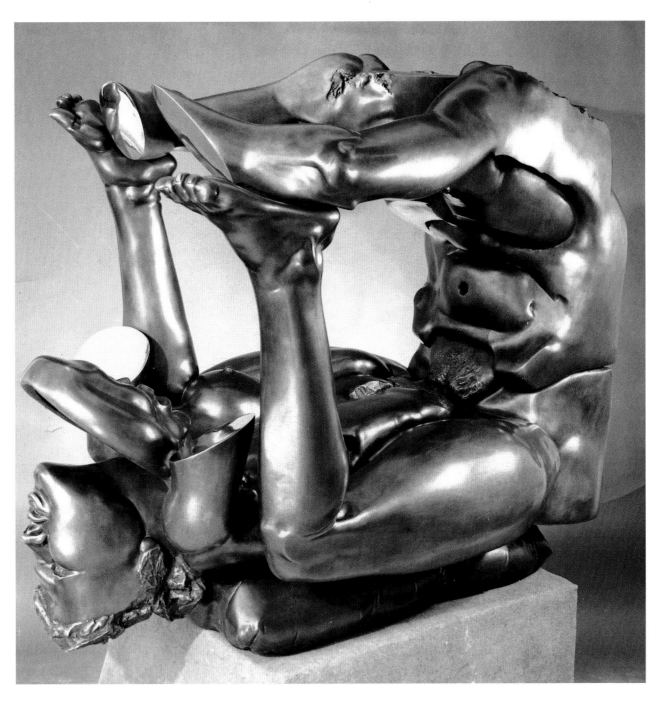

IPOUSTEGUY *La Maison* (front)
Galerie Claude Bernard, Paris

and female arms are broken smoothly, their polished stumps cut off like limbs passing beyond the edge of a canvas. The two interlocked bodies form a structural rectangle, the *maison* of the title, making the witty point that our households are founded on copulation. The wit does not vitiate the grandeur, however, of the muscular forms, nor the curious agony of the contorted pose, the headless and handless man like some male insect being consumed in the sex act, and his sexual partner showing two visages—an eyeless social mask lifted in blank confrontation, an inner face bent back in orgasmic ecstasy. Ipoustéguy has described one of the characteristics of his work as *"l'anatomie des hommes mêlée à une sorte d'environment"*—"human anatomy mixed up with a sort of environment"—and in *Maison* the environmental house is conveyed not only by the cushions beneath the female's back and the wall-like smoothness of the male's back but by the squared-off intimacy, the private chamber, of the rectangular pose. *"Mes personnages sont toujours en train de se conjuguer avec des formes géométriques, architecturales"* ("My figures are always linking themselves with geometrical, architectural forms").

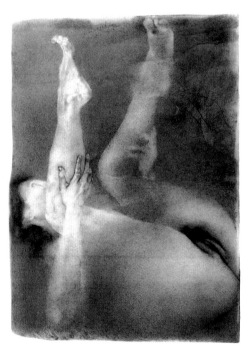

IPOUSTEGUY
V, 1976
Charcoal and crayon, 35 × 26″
Galerie Claude Bernard, Paris

The female's extremely flexible and submissive position in *Maison*, forming right angles, was anticipated in a crayon drawing of 1975, and echoed in an erotic cycle of charcoals in 1978–79; the artist's desire to explore and bring to light the site of our births goes beyond libido into a realm of stoic compassion. *La Naissance* is as polished and iconic as one of Brancusi's "eggs" and yet as anatomical as a medical book. The slight asymmetry of the helpless feet, the delicate symmetry of the exposed anus, the impression of contrasting strengths given by the female thighs and ministering male arms, the emerging fetal cranium—these are movingly human, at a base level seldom touched by art. This sculpture, brought to a rare polish and purity, with none of the broken seams and rough overlappings with which the sculptor customarily qualifies his nudes, has been linked, surprisingly, by Ipoustéguy to *Homme poussant la porte: "Bien d'autres de mes sculptures ont dit cette poussée vitale, cette percée. . . . Ainsi* La Naissance *comme une boulet hors du corps. J'ai toujours cherché à exalter, par le mythe, la pulsion vitale. Ainsi dans* L'Homme poussant la porte, *je pousse la porte, je pousse la tête, j'entre dans la vie. En luttant contre les agres-*

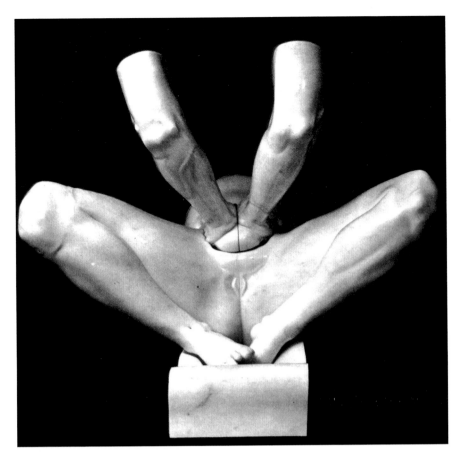

Ipousteguy
La Naissance, 1968
Marble, 39½ × 35½ × 31½″
Galerie Claude Bernard, Paris

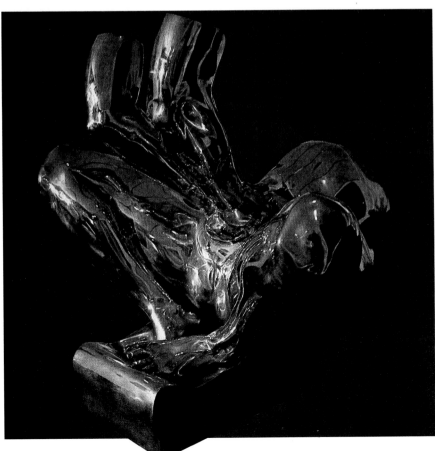

Ipousteguy
La Naissance, 1968
Bronze, 33 × 37½ × 29½″
Galerie Claude Bernard, Paris

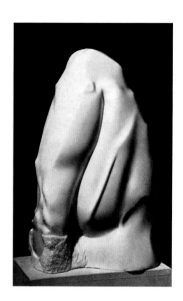

IPOUSTEGUY
Le Grand Coude
Marble, 25 1/2 × 15 3/4 × 9″
Galerie Claude Bernard, Paris

sions de la vie par une agression en retour. Pour me venger de ce qui m'agresse" ("Others of my sculptures have expressed this vital push, this breakthrough. . . . Thus, *Birth* like a cannonball out of the body. I have always sought to exalt, by means of myth, the vital drive. Just as in *Man Pushing the Door* I push the door, I push the head, I enter into life. In wrestling against the attacks of life by an attack in return. In order to revenge myself against that which attacks me"). The corroded, cankered, and broken textures which interrupt the skinlike smoothness of his surfaces witness a wrestling, then, between vitality and its enemies; another sort of environment, that of Darwinian struggle and ravaging Time, is *mêlée* with *l'anatomie des hommes*. The human body in its heroic vulnerability underlies the marvellous array of Ipoustéguy's substances and styles. Of his erotic works, he has said, "*Ce sont les fruits des expériences de mon corps. De mon vécu sensuel. Toute œuvre vient du corps et y revient*" ("They are the fruit of experiences of my own body. Of my sensual truth. All work comes from the body and returns there").

Pieces of anatomy imply a vital force that the complete form has become too trite to embody; corporeality authenticates itself through duplicated, severed, and transmuted parts. Ipoustéguy has produced sculptures of discrete hands and feet and breasts and legs, of an isolated elbow (*Grand Coude,* 1978), vulva (*Triptyque,* 1976), heart (*Le Cœur,* 1966), and brain (*L'Encéphale,* 1960). *La Mort du père* (*The Death of the Father,* 1969) distributes around a central grieving figure holding a sculptor's mallet ten pillowed heads, wearing papal mitres, in a rich range of cheesy, bony transformation; sepulchral art also acknowledges, with a devastating honesty, the truth of the body. Ipoustéguy's sculptural humanism cannot overlook the well-publicized fragmented, disconnected, anxious, and morbid condition of twentieth-century man. Yet, as John Ashbery has pointed out, in one of the remarkably few useful comments written in English (for the catalogue of a London show in 1964) on this masterly post-modern sculptor, his work quite lacks the elegiac quality present in that of Brancusi, Moore, and Giacometti, where "a hidden despair subsists." Ashbery points out, "There is none in Ipoustéguy: not that you could call him positive, but there is simply neither room nor time for it—his figures are totally occupied with living out the role that their forms assign to them."

Ipoustéguy's baroque virtuosity, his Renaissance excitement over human anatomy, his worn and battered textures, and his anecdotal titles

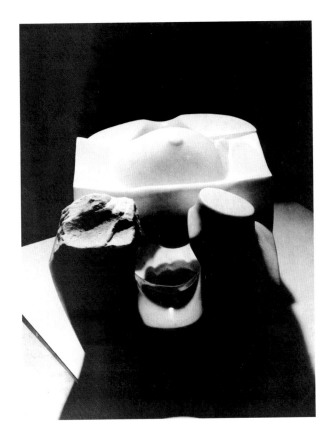

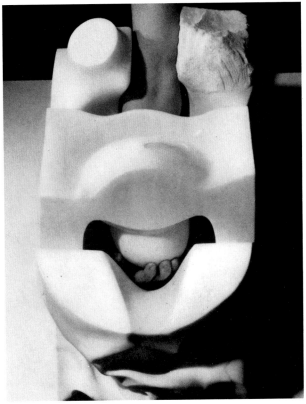

have all been revived from pre-modern times, yet something unnervingly futuristic haunts his willful conjurations in marble and bronze. They hang on the edge of a world devoid of judgments. His sculptures refuse to submit to any academic or anti-academic idea; his clownishness, like Picasso's, answers to the exuberance of Nature. The complexity of the organic—*vivantes contradictions!*—empowers him. His hand collaborates with inhuman forces that roughen and smooth. The glossy and lewd *Sein tactile* (*Tactile Breast,* 1968) but emphasizes the tactility that pervades his creation; we wish to touch his works, much as we itch to touch other bodies, because their textures are not monotonous but responsive and various. Ipoustéguy's sculpture offers the metamorphic intimacy of natural encounter, in substances of classic durance.

IPOUSTEGUY
(Left) *Sein tactile,* 1968
Marble, 26 × 14 × 14″
Galerie Claude Bernard, Paris

(Right) *Sein tactile* being tactilely appreciated
Galerie Claude Bernard, Paris

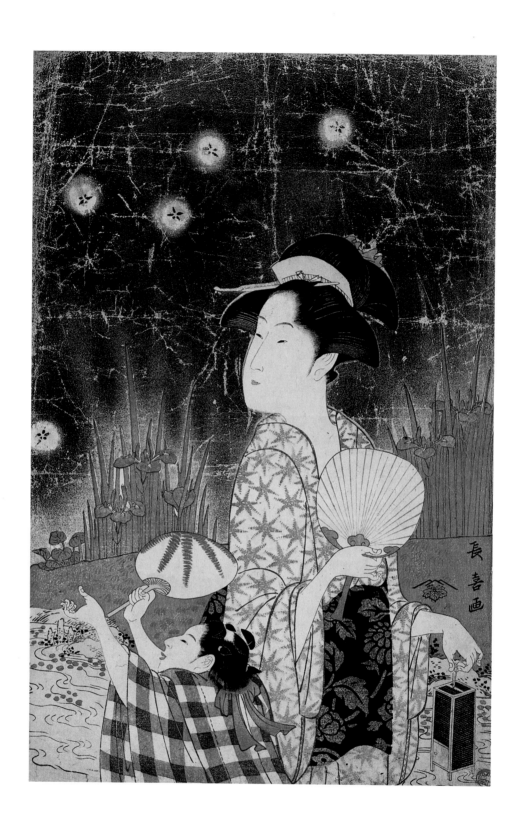

Little Lightnings

———

THE BACKYARDS of my boyhood in summer were full of fireflies, but now I see them rarely. Is it that I have moved a few degrees north, or are the fireflies a quiet victim of the same environmental withering that has stolen the purple martins and the box turtles from our everyday lives? Or do I no longer look for them, with the delight depicted here?

Here, in eighteenth-century Japan, the young mother holds an exquisite little slatted box ready for their capture. In my Depression Pennsylvania, a pickle jar had to do, with holes punched in the lid and some grass lining the bottom, for the comfort of the captives. They were easy to catch, the obliging lightning bugs—soft-winged beetles that seldom rose higher than a child's hand could reach. In the palm, they lit up the creases with their cool yellow glow, whose rhythm seemed a kind of bleating.

Were they frightened? I imagined so, though the tempo of their bright pulse did not increase. If science can be believed, the signal is erotic, male to female and back again—like notes passed back and forth in class, like blushes or those dilations of the pupil that betray human arousal—and it is produced by an infusion of air through cells whose subtle load of luciferin becomes oxyluciferin, the oxygen catalyzed by luciferase.

As my elders, not disapproving, sat back in the dark of the lawn, smoking their cigars and murmuring their gossip and making the wicker furniture squeak, I acted the wanton tyrant amid this docile glimmering race.

CHŌKI
Catching Fireflies, mid-1790s
"Brocade" woodblock print
on paper, 10 × 15"
The British Museum,
Department of Oriental
Antiquities, London

The fireflies in my imagination were afraid; their blinking constituted a plea to be set free, and usually they were, thankfully resuming their ornamental swim through the shadows of the trees, above the dew of the lawn. But once, with the clumsiness of a child, I knocked a firefly to the earth, or pinched it and let it fall, and in attempting to rescue it—to dig it up from between the blades of grass—I only poked it deeper. Horrified, I beheld its abdomen glimmering, finally, out. This death, which I had both caused and witnessed, haunted me in giant proportions. I did not know, as the encyclopedia tells me now, that "adult fireflies of many species do not feed"; that they exist to mate, to engender larvae which feed on snails and earthworms, "injecting their prey with a paralyzing fluid"; that the firefly, in short, whose death I caused was already dying, enjoying a mere momentary sexual dance between one generation of poisonous larvae and the next—already enjoying a kind of afterlife.

The boy and his mother seem to understand this, in this woodblock print by Chōki. They inhabit a kind of heaven, economical as a memory. Neither the running brook nor the listening iris protest their attempt to catch a few stars. Oddly, the one element of this print to show the effects of age is the ageless night itself—the purplish background of *sumi* and mica, creased and scuffed as if with little lightnings.

Heavily Hyped Helga

ONE MUST approach the Helga exhibition determined to forgive it its hype. For months before the show arrived in Boston, subway riders were tantalized by posters saying, "To the world, she has become a sensation. To Wyeth, she was just the girl next door."

What does one do with the girl next door? Why, one falls in love with her, and, if one is an artist of a certain stripe, paints and draws her, mostly in the nude, over two hundred times over a period of fifteen years, amassing a collection that is then bought by a millionaire collector like Leonard E. B. Andrews, publisher of such pivotal newsletters as *The National Bankruptcy Report* and *The Swine Flu Claim & Litigation Reporter,* who seals the transaction with a handshake and the mural-scale remark, "Mr. Wyeth, congratulations, you have created a national treasure, and I want to protect it and show it to the American people. I want the collection." In confirmation of Mr. Andrews's generous estimate, a portrait of Helga adorned simultaneous covers of *Time* and *Newsweek* in August of 1986, and in May of 1987 a show mounted at the National Gallery, with a best-selling catalogue introduced by the Gallery's Deputy Director John Wilmerding, began a continental circuit to museums in Boston, Houston, Los Angeles, San Francisco, and Detroit.

The nub of the stir that the Helga collection has made is the innuendo, not exactly suppressed by Betsy Wyeth's blaming it all on "love," that its hitherto unexhibited riches record a secret love affair. Not only is Helga Testorf, a Chadds Ford neighbor of the Wyeths, often rendered in the nude, but she is painted dozing in a rumpled bed, in a little whitewashed room like that of an olde-tyme motel, or with a black riband around her neck in deliberate echo of the loose lady in Manet's *Olympia*. That global excitement could be generated by the dim possibility that an aging artist had slept with his middle-aged model (Wyeth was fifty-three when the sequence began in 1971, and Helga was fifty-three when it ended in 1985) testifies, I suppose, to the lowered sexual expectations of the AIDS era; those of us who were young in the Fifties sympathetically recall how a little (a glimpse of Hedy Lamarr's breasts in *Ecstasy;* Brigitte Bardot's bottom in the middle distance of *And God Created Woman*) can be made to go a long way. Idle speculation about the artist and his model predates the tale of Pygmalion and Galatea; the Victorians worried a good deal about the erotic potential of the studio, and Thomas Eakins's painting of the artist William Rush extending a courteous hand to his naked model as she descends from the draped platform is rich with anxiety—his, hers, and ours. But in fact none of the Helga paintings, intensely worked and radiantly real as some are, forms quite the sunburst of female glory un-veiled by Wyeth's 1969 *Virgin*, of the then fifteen-year-old Siri Erikson.

Helga, with her thick braids, heavy features, and sour expression, is somewhat plain, which quickens our titillated suspicions: if she isn't a beauty, why are her clothes off? The Helga pictures also show her, like a Playmate of the Month, engaged in healthy outdoor activities—walking in a loden coat, brooding amid the sticks and dead leaves of Wyeth's cus-tomary wintry landscape. In Boston, the exhibit—set up as if *sub rosa* in some galleries emptied of their usual Chinese art, while the Museum of Fine Art's premier exhibition space, the Gund Gallery, has been given over to a retrospective of the chastely mechanistic Charles Sheeler—has been arranged rather like a striptease, with the pencilled head-studies and the muffled loden-coat watercolors yielding around a corner to rooms of nudity. Helga's body, first seen when she is thirty-eight and last when she is over fifty, is a remarkably firm one, and in many of its representations might be that of a young girl. And perhaps that sufficiently explains her charm for the artist.

The mood of the portraits is elusive. Often deadpan Helga is not so much there as her hair is there, braided or free-flowing or cut in a pageboy, each glowing filament laid on, in the more finished works, in painstaking

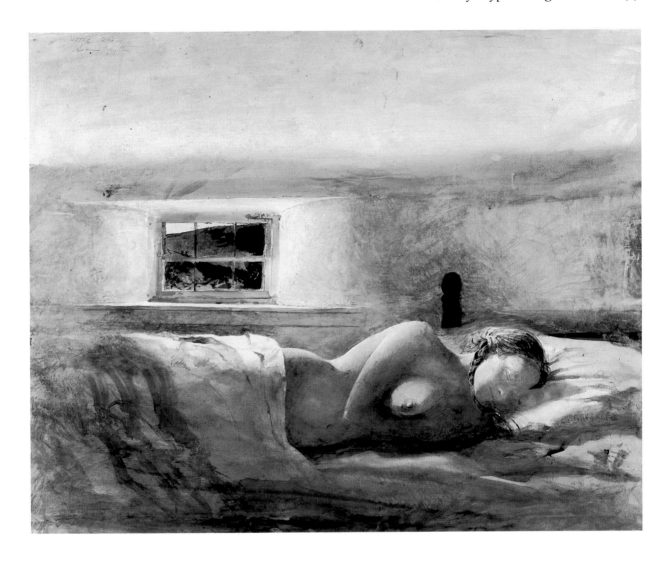

tempera or drybrush—a miracle of eyesight if not of mimesis. "What's drybrush?" art-viewers kept asking each other the day I viewed the show. It is a technique whereby a watercolor brush is squeezed almost dry to produce a fine, opaque line. Mr. Wilmerding's introduction relates how Wyeth was captivated by this technique in the work of Albrecht Dürer, and Helga in *Sheepskin* does look Düreresque—flattened and enamelled and darkened as if by centuries. Dürer's virtually microscopic rendering of a hare's coat, or the grasses in a piece of turf, has about it, though, the Renaissance exhilaration of recovering the physical world: not for a thou-

ANDREW WYETH
Study for *Overflow,* 1975
Watercolor, 22³/₄ × 28³/₄″
All the works of Wyeth shown here reproduced courtesy of Ann Kendall Richards, Inc., New York

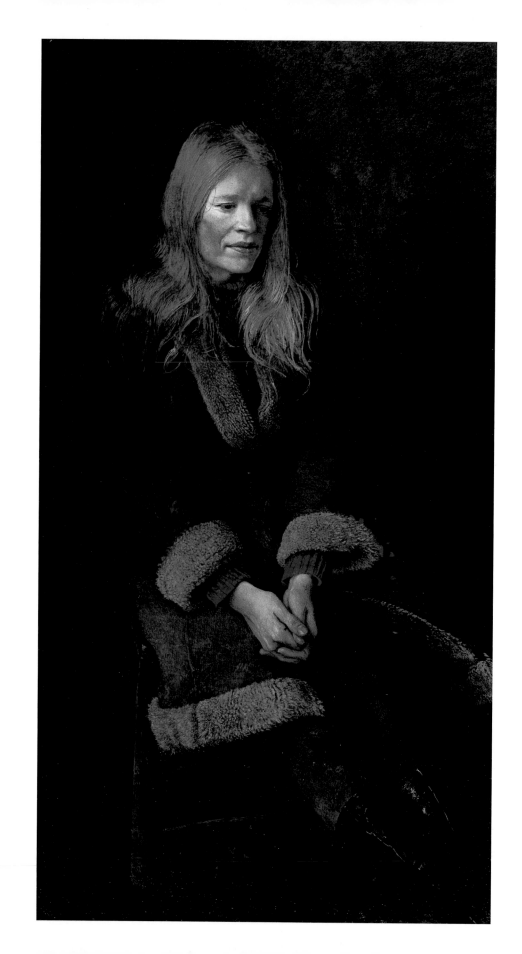

sand years had things seemed so interesting in themselves; never, before Dürer and Leonardo, had reality been so exactly captured in drawing. With a late-twentieth-century artist like Wyeth, such close and avid rendering of hair, fur, thready sweaters, and eyelashes—in hyperfinished, minutely mottled paintings like *Braids* and *The Prussian,* even the skin looks reconstructed, squamous cell by squamous cell—amounts to a knowing defiance, one underlined by the broad and scrubby contrasting sections that seem to say, "I can be abstract, too!" The catalogue chapters are headed by remarks that, however extracted from Wyeth, seem here a bit self-serving and apologetic. "I honestly consider myself an abstractionist. . . . My people, my objects, breathe in a different way; there's another core—an excitement that's definitely abstract." The slashes of daylight behind the figure in *Drawn Shade* could have come from a Franz Kline, and two of the finest reclining nudes (*Black Velvet,* supine, and *Nudes,* prone) float in a pure mess of dark-brown brushstrokes.

Of course, dashingly rough rendering toward the edges can be found

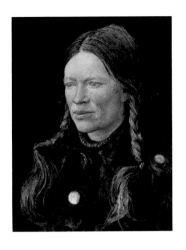

WYETH
The Prussian (detail), 1973
Drybrush, 29¹/₂ × 21¹/₂″

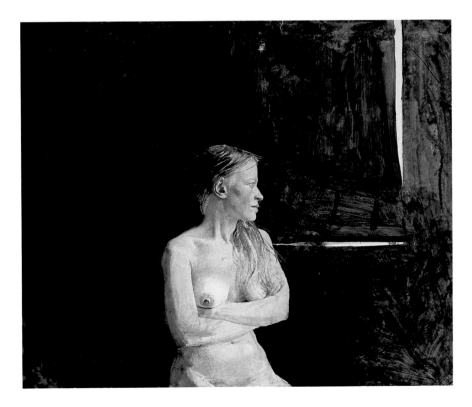

WYETH
(Opposite) *Sheepskin,* 1972
Tempera, 33³/₈ × 18″

(Left) *Drawn Shade,* 1976
Drybrush and watercolor,
23 × 28″

in magazine illustrations, and it is Wyeth's ties, filial and geographical, to the Philadelphia tradition of commercial illustration that incite such vehement scorn among aesthetic arbiters like Hilton Kramer, Henry Geldzahler, and, more politely, Robert Hughes. In the heyday of Abstract Expressionism, the scorn was simple gallery politics, but resistance to Wyeth remains curiously stiff in an art world that has no trouble making room for Photorealists like Richard Estes and Philip Pearlstein and William Bailey and Jack Beal and graduates of commercial art like Wayne Thiebaud, Andy Warhol, and, for that matter, Edward Hopper. We resent broody poses in Wyeth and accept them from Hopper, perhaps because

WYETH
Nudes, 1981
Watercolor, 18 1/8 × 24″

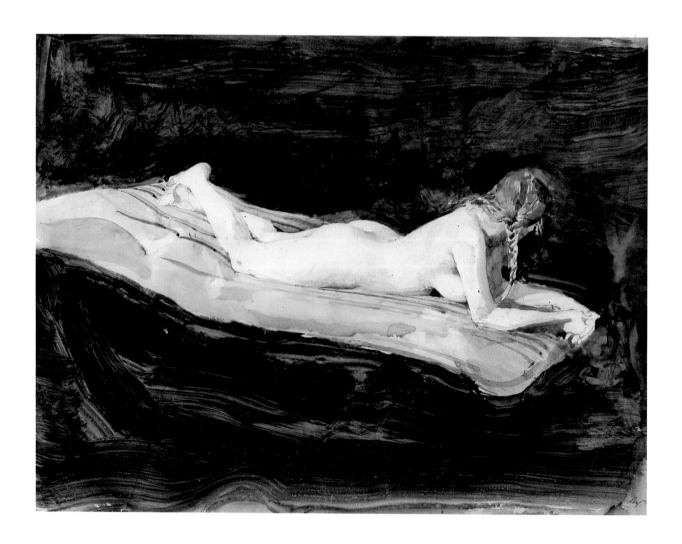

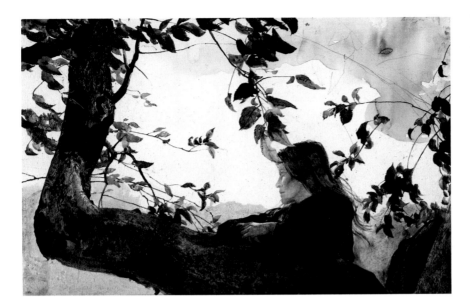

WYETH
In the Orchard, 1974
Watercolor and traces of pencil,
19³/₄ × 29³/₄"

there is a glamorizing touch in a Wyeth painting like *In the Orchard* and none in a Hopper like *Morning Sun,* or because broodiness feels more excusable in Hopper's urban than in Wyeth's rural settings. Nevertheless, the two men are close—close in their loyalty to American landscape and in their interest in the thoughtful light at the edges of the day—and posterity may wonder how one could be so "in" and the other so "out."

At the exhibition, my own pleasure did diminish whenever I felt Wyeth was trying to tell me a story, as with the tricky little illumined spillage through the window above the sleeping nude in *Overflow* (she is dreaming of overflow? she has just been overflowed into?), or when he was using light theatrically (*Night Shadow; Sun Shield*), or when he dressed Helga up in costumes like a doll (*Peasant Dress; Crown of Flowers*). Wyeth has, I think, an intense and individual enough relation to his visual material not to need to toy with it. A painting such as *Farm Road,* for instance, with its massive, shining back of a braided head bluntly centered in a scratchy brown monotone beneath a tilted horizon and a fused clump of pines, wins an expressionistic strangeness not from any anecdotal overtones but from the absorbed way it is painted. Here, and elsewhere, something has been released by Helga's turning her back. The liveliest portraits in the show, the ones that least effortfully deliver a sense of spirit

WYETH
Overflow, 1976
Drybrush, 23 × 29″

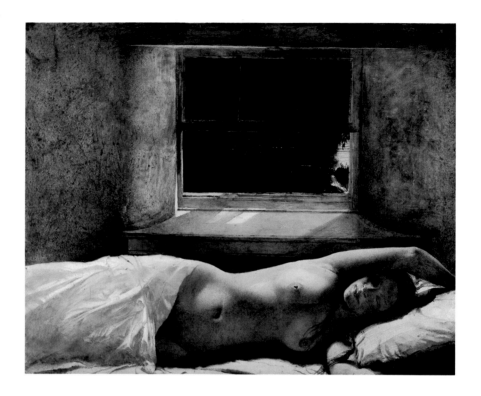

WYETH
Her Daughter, 1971
Watercolor and traces of pencil,
21 5/8 × 30″

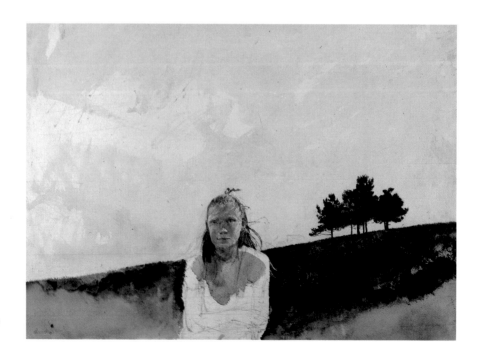

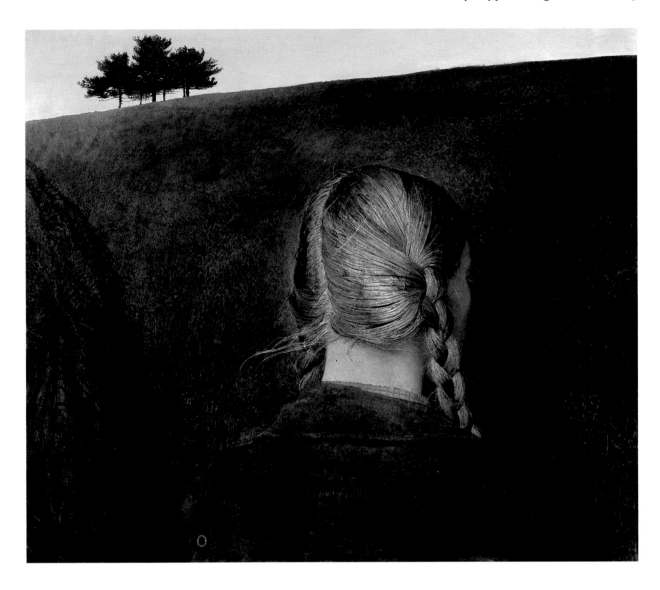

in a face, are a few of Helga's pre-adolescent daughter; the girl has an elfin, skewed look the artist easily captures, relieved of his chronic subject's impassive gravity.

The show mounts less than half of Mr. Andrews's national treasure, yet even so seems somewhat thin and repetitious; my fellow viewers, having been satisfied as to what drypoint is, politely stooped toward each fragmentary sketch like salesmen dutifully knocking on a row of unopening

WYETH
Farm Road, 1979
Tempera, $21 \times 25^{1}/_{4}''$

Wyeth   Pencil studies:
(top left) *Asleep*, 1975,
18 × 23 3/4"; (top right)
Overflow, 1976, 18 3/4 × 24 5/8";
(bottom left) *Overflow*, 1976,
25 5/8 × 36 1/2"; (bottom right)
Barracoon, 1976, 18 × 23 3/4"

doors. Yet the high points do represent, it seems to me, an expansion of Wyeth's artistic ambition, and should expand his reputation beyond that of a dryly meticulous renderer of dead grasses, barn walls, and withered country characters. My personal method for locating high points is a simple one: the covetousness test. Would I want to own it and see it daily? A number of the pencil sketches met that test: the entire *Asleep* sequence and the studies for *Overflow, Black Velvet,* and *Barracoon* have a cumulative power as Helga driftingly turns this way and that. The pose (or fact)

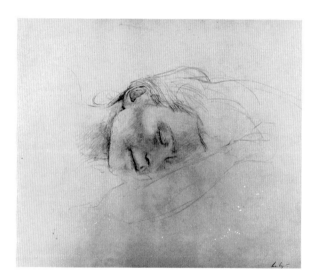

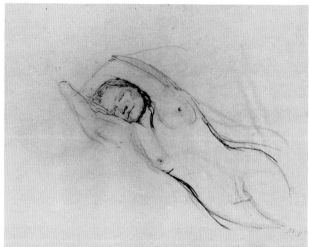

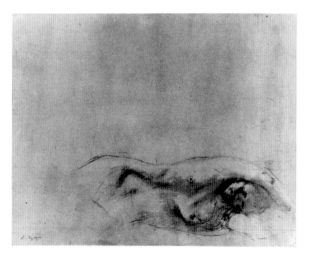

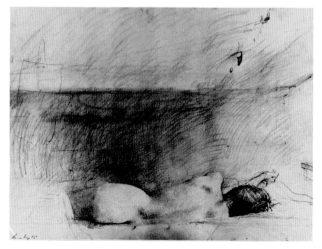

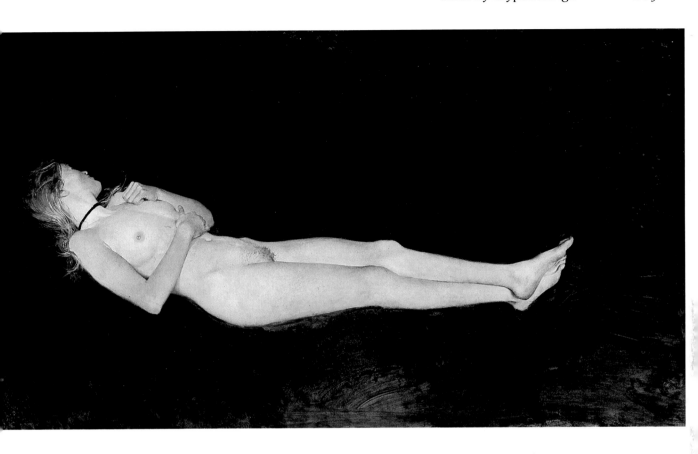

of sleep somehow lifts these nude studies beyond both academic and erotic anxiousness and irradiates their physical intimacy with auras from the realm of Blake and Jung. We sense here what Wyeth means when he says, "I enter in a very focused way and then I go through it." Of the other pencil works, the very first sketch of Helga, in profile, has an unforced nobility, and in those posed with the dog Nell the dog's company lends her face an unusual expression of amusement. Here, and in numbers 116 and 129 of the sleeping model, the sometimes staid linear precision is animated by a visible scribbling, an energy in the pencil.

Among the finished paintings, *Black Velvet* seemed to me a triumph: a long nude, tawny white, reclines in space as black as the velvet ribbon around her neck. She is an American Venus, with something touchingly gawky in her beautifully drawn big bare feet, bent elbow, and clenched hands. This is what Winslow Homer's maidens would have looked like

WYETH
Black Velvet, 1972
Drybrush, $21^{1}/_{4} \times 39^{1}/_{4}"$

beneath their calico. Looser in rendering, and less arbitrarily afloat, upon an inflated plastic raft in what seems a very muddy pond, *Nudes* takes the saucy bottoms-up position of a Boucher; it, and the larger and more finished of the watercolors titled *From the Back*, possess what is often absent from Wyeth's showpieces—a sense of massiness, of sculptural shadow and of potential motion. *From the Back* catches a rough-hewn giantess as she swingingly strides into a darkness that swallows her arm. Both these, and the perhaps slightly too monumental *Lovers*, were done in 1981, and display an unfussy confidence with the nude, and an underlying humor, that Wyeth achieved over his instinctive dryness. The finished *On Her Knees* (an erotically charged pose that he has used several times elsewhere) seems to me to suffer from this dryness, a studied grainy glamour, but in the same series the headless, breastless, armless abdomen, with its honestly thick waist and tangled pubic hair thrusting flamelike above a phallic shadow, confronts us—affronts us, even—as if still wet from the artist's brush. And the painting *Barracoon* (a word for slave-barracks suggested by Betsy Wyeth, and also produced in a version where the sleeping woman has been colored black) is as graceful as its pose is perennial and more delicate, in its hippy rhythm, than the often reproduced back view of a reclining nude by John Trumball.

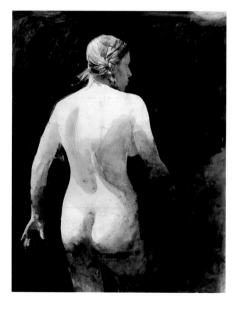

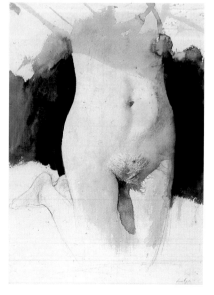

WYETH
(Left) *From the Back*, 1981
Watercolor, 23 3/4 × 18 5/8"

(Right) *On Her Knees*, 1977
Watercolor and traces of pencil,
29 7/8 × 21 3/8"

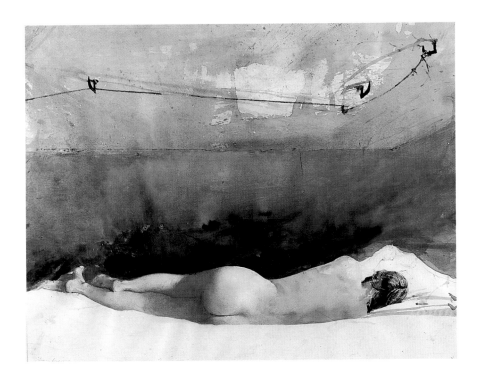

WYETH
Barracoon, 1976
Drybrush and watercolor,
$19^{3}/_{4} \times 25^{1}/_{8}''$

The nudes are what make the show sensational, and also what make it worthwhile. They significantly add to a venerable genre rather undernourished in America, where the menace and sadness of naked flesh have impressed artists as much as its grandeur and allure. When all the hype has faded, and Leonard Andrews has got his (to cite the rumored purchase price) ten million dollars' worth of exposure, Wyeth's fifteen years of friendly interest in Helga should leave a treasurable residue.

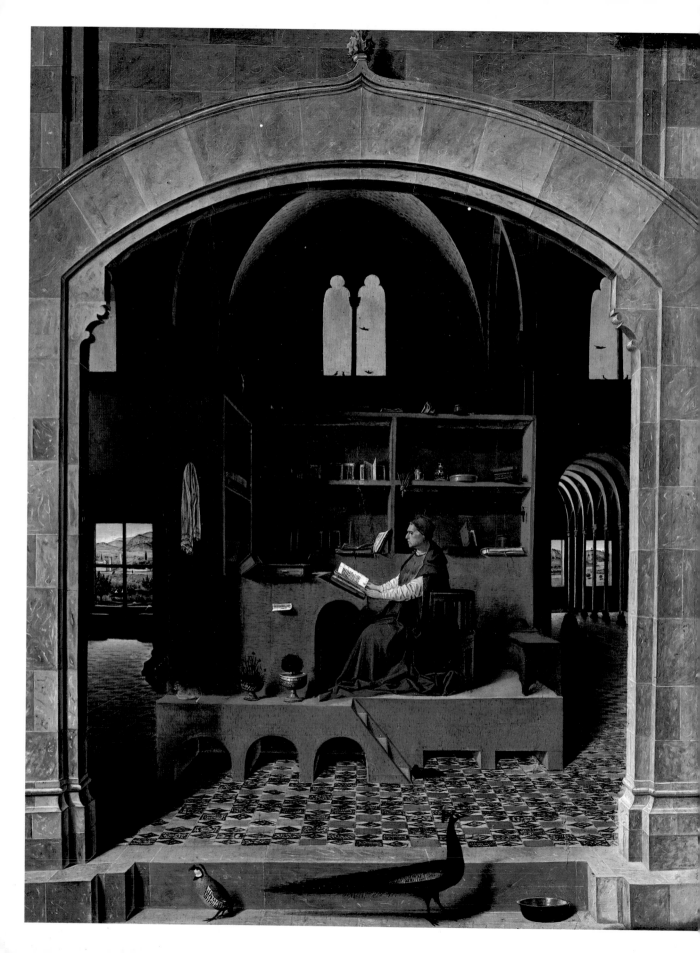

Working Space

SAINT JEROME in his study would appear to be well set up. A platform three steps high lifts him off the chilly floor. The chest at his back is about to fall off the edge with a crash, but it probably contains only unsolicited homilies and courtesy copies of first polemics. The light, though a little theatrical, looks steady, and is coming from the left. The shelving on his right is a good idea, though apparently unadjustable. He has tacked up where it can't be lost in the shuffle a slip of parchment, perhaps a favorite quote from Origen or the germ idea for a new attack on the Pelagians. Small wonder he produced here the millennium's best-seller, the *Vulgate*. All these stout brown arches seem constructed to give him shelter and peace, and the many lines of perspective allegorize the calm convergences of a meditating brain.

But those birds at the window must be noisy, not to mention the peacock and the quail staging a lovers' quarrel in the foreground. The books around him are rather dishevelled, his reading of many evidently broken off in the middle. Who is going to feed the cat? And what is this approaching over on the right, in shadow? As ominous as Francis Bacon's famous dog, it appears to be an emaciated lion dipped in black. From its eager expression and gingerly tread, it has a thorn in its foot it wants removed. Saint Jerome is about to suffer the fate of every saint and sinner in his study. He is about to be interrupted.

ANTONELLO DA MESSINA
St. Jerome in His Study,
c. 1457–74
Oil on wood, 18 × 14 1/2″
The National Gallery, London

Writers and Artists

—————

THE ITCH to make dark marks on white paper is shared by writers and artists. Before the advent of the typewriter and now the word processor, pen and ink were what one drew pictures and word-pictures with; James Joyce, who let others do his typing, said he liked to feel the words flow through his wrist.

There is a graphic beauty to old manuscripts, and to the signatures whose flourishes and curlicues were meant to discourage forgery. The manuscripts of Ouida, dashed off with, it seems, an ostrich quill, and the strenuously hatched and interlineated manuscripts of Pope and Boswell are as much pictorial events as a diploma by Steinberg. An old-fashioned gentleman's skills often included the ability to limn a likeness or a landscape, much as middle-class men now can all operate a camera; such writers as Pushkin and Goethe startle us with the competence of their sketches.

Thackeray, of course, was a professional illustrator, as were Beerbohm and Evelyn Waugh. Edward Lear was a serious painter and a frivolous writer, and he might be surprised to know that the writing has won him posterity's ticket. On the other hand, Wyndham Lewis now seems to be valued more for his edgy portraits of his fellow modernists than for his once much-admired prose. Thurber was thought of as a writer who, comically and touchingly, could not draw but did anyway, whereas Lud-

OUIDA
(MARIE LOUISE DE LA RAMEE)
Detail of MS of *Tonia* (c. 1890)
Ink on paper, actual size
Beinecke Rare Book and
Manuscript Library,
Yale University

ALEXANDER POPE   Page of MS of *Essay on Man* (1733–34). Ink on paper, 9 × 6″
Harvard University Library and the Pierpont Morgan Library

JOHANN WOLFGANG VON GOETHE
*The Chapel of St. Lawrence in
Karlsbad,* 1808
Pen and ink with sepia wash,
4 ¹/₄ × 5 ³/₄"
The Goethe Museums,
Düsseldorf

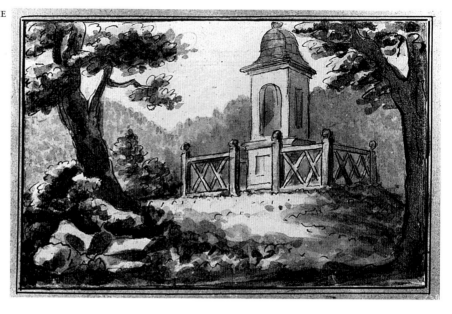

wig Bemelmans is remembered, if he is remembered at all, as an artist
who could write, mostly about hotels; in truth, both men were bold mini-
malists in an era when cartoons were executed in sometimes suffocating
detail. A number of writers began as cartoonists: of S. J. Perelman we
might have suspected this, and even of Gabriel García Márquez; but Flannery O'Connor? Yes, when we think of her vivid outrageousness, her primary colors, the sharpness of her every stroke. In "The Fiction Writer and
His Country" she decreed, "To the hard of hearing you shout, and for the
almost-blind you draw large and startling figures."

Alphabets begin in pictographs, and, though words are spoken things,
to write and read we must see. The line between picture and symbol is a
fine one. In the days of mass illiteracy, imagery—hung on cathedral walls,
scattered in woodcuts—was the chief non-oral narrative means. Most
paintings "tell a story," and even departures from representation carry a
literary residue; e.g., the labels and bits of newspaper worked into Cubist
collages, and the effect of a monumental calligraphy in the canvases of
Pollock and Kline. The art of the comic strip exists as if to show how small
the bridge need be between the two forms of showing, of telling. Music,
perhaps the most ancient of the fine arts, is simultaneously more visceral

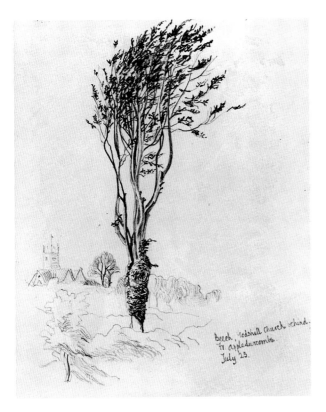

(Left) GERARD MANLEY HOPKINS
Beech, Godshill Church Behind, 1863
Pencil on paper, $11 \times 8\frac{1}{2}''$
Harry Ransom Humanities Research Center Art
Collection, The University of Texas at Austin

(Below left) EDGAR ALLAN POE
Portrait of Elmira Royster Shelton, 1845. Crayon, $11 \times 8\frac{3}{4}''$
Lilly Library, Indiana University, Bloomington, Indiana

(Below right) OSCAR WILDE
Portrait of Florence Balcombe, 1876. Pencil, $6\frac{7}{8} \times 4\frac{7}{8}''$
Harry Ransom Humanities Research Center Art Collection,
The University of Texas at Austin

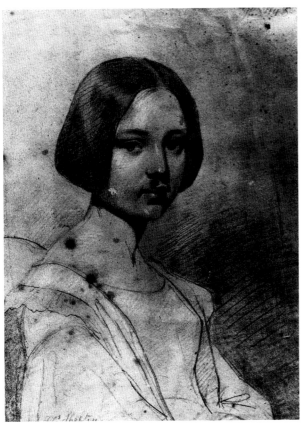

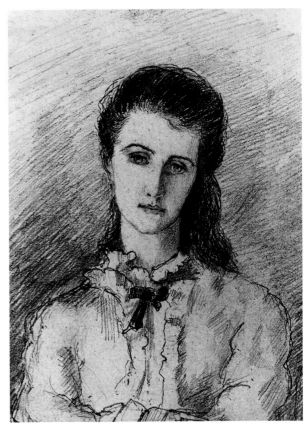

(Near right)
WYNDHAM LEWIS
T. S. Eliot, 1949
Charcoal pencil, 22 × 13″
Harry Ransom Humanities
Research Center Art Collection,
The University of Texas
at Austin

(Far right)
O. HENRY
Mr. Hog, c. 1892
Pencil with watercolor wash on
notepad paper, 8 1/2 × 5″
Harry Ransom Humanities
Research Center Art Collection,
The University of Texas
at Austin

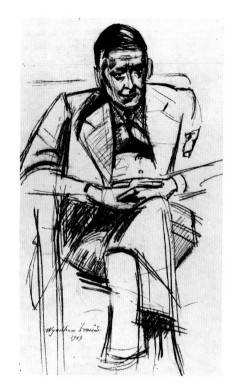

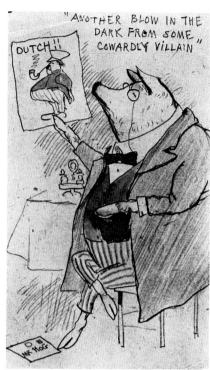

and abstract, and though some musicians become writers (John Barth, Anthony Burgess) the leap is rarer. Music is a world of its own; writing and drawing are relatively parasitic upon the world that is in place.

As those who have both drawn and written know, the problems of definition differ radically. A table or a person becomes in graphic representation a maze of angles, of half-hidden bulges, of second and third and fourth looks adding up to an illusion of thereness. When color is added to line, the decisions and discriminations freighted into each square inch approach the infinite; one's eyes begin to hurt, to water, and the colors on the palette converge toward gray mud. Whereas the writer only has to say "table" to put it there, on the page. Everything in the way of adjectival adjustment doesn't so much add as carve away at the vague shape the word, all by itself, has conjured up. To make the table convincing, a specified color, wood, or number of legs might be helpful; or it might be too much, an overparticularized clot in the flow of the prose. The reader, encountering the word "table," has, hastily and hazily, supplied one from his

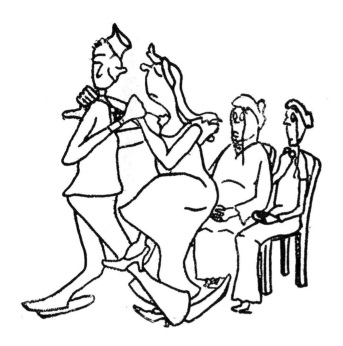

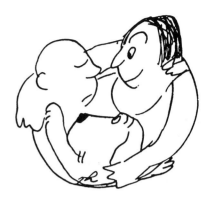

experience, and particularization risks diminishing, rather than adding to, the reality of the table in his mind. Further, the table takes meaning and mass from its context of human adventure. It must tell us something about the human being who owns or uses it, his or her financial or social or moral condition; otherwise this piece of furniture exists outside the movement of the story and is merely "painterly."

The painter's media are palpable. The more he tells us, the more we know. What he tells us, goes: his strokes are here and not there, this and not that. Although I rarely have cause in my adult life to open the India-ink bottle, when I do, and take the feather-light nib and holder again in hand, and begin to trace wet marks over my pencil sketch on the pristine Bristol board, the old excitement returns—the glistening quick precision, the possibility of smudging, the tremor and swoop that impart life to the lines. Drawing, we dip directly into physical reality. The child discovers that a few dots and a curved line will do for a face, which smiles back out at him. Something has been generated from nothing. Or the pose of a mo-

(Above left)
FLANNERY O'CONNOR
Cartoon of *Naval Training Program at Georgia College for Women*, c. 1944
Woodblock print on paper, 3 × 3″

(Above right)
JAMES THURBER
Man, Woman, and Dog, 1943
Pen and ink, 2 × 2″
Collection of Helen Thurber and Rosemary Thurber

ment has been set down forever; back in my mother's attic, old sketchpads of mine hold pets long dead, infants now grown to adulthood, grandparents whose voices I will not hear again.

Years before written words become pliant and expressive to their young user, creative magic can be grasped through pen and ink, brush and paint. The subtleties of form and color, the distinctions of texture, the balances of volume, the principles of perspective and composition—all these are good for a future writer to explore and will help him to visualize his scenes, even to construct his personalities and to shape the invisible contentions and branchings of plot. A novel, like a cartoon, arranges stylized versions of people within a certain space: the graphic artist learns to organize and emphasize, and this knowledge serves the writer. The tinted volumes that confront the outer eye—that most vulnerable of body parts, where our brain interfaces with the world—are imitated by those dramatic spaces the inner eye creates, as theatres for thoughts and fantasies.

JOHN UPDIKE
(Below right)
Cartoon from *The Harvard Lampoon*, 1953

(Below left)
Spot drawing from *The Harvard Lampoon*, 1953

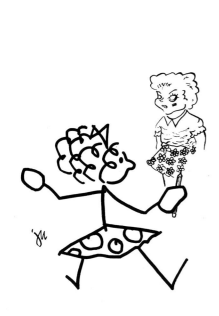

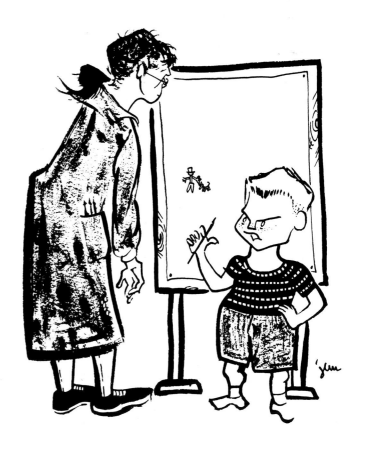

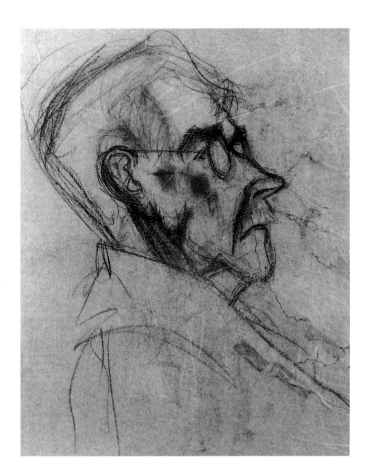

UPDIKE
John Franklin Hoyer, c. 1952
Charcoal on back of gray
drawing pad cover, scored by
dog claws, 17³/₄ × 20¹/₂″
Private collection

Whether painting or imagining a scene, one tries to "sink in" and to induce harmonies to reveal themselves, amid a pervasive increase of clarity.

Joseph Conrad, introducing his third novel, the novel that committed
him to the writer's vocation, made the visual component central: "Art
itself may be defined as a single-minded attempt to render the highest
kind of justice to the visible universe. . . . It is an attempt to find in its
forms, in its colors, in its light, in its shadows, in the aspects of matter and
in the facts of life, what of each is fundamental, what is enduring and
essential. . . . My task which I am trying to achieve is, by the power of the
written word, to make you hear, to make you feel—it is, before all, to
make you *see*."

"The highest kind of justice to the visible universe"—the phrase, extrapolated to include "psychological" and "social" along with "visible," idealistically sums up what the poet and storyteller hope to render. As training to render such justice, no better school exists than graphic representation, with its striving for accuracy, vivacity, and economy. Small wonder that writers, so many of them, have drawn and painted: the tools are allied, the impulse is one.

Credits

page 37   KATE GREENAWAY: From *Kate Greenaway's Birthday Book*. Photograph: Robert D. Rubíc

38   EDWARD LEAR: "Manypeeplia Upsidownia" from *Nonsense Songs, Stories, Botany, and Alphabets*. Photograph: Robert D. Rubic

39   N. C. WYETH: *The Flight Across the Lake*. Reproduced by permission of Charles Scribner's Sons, an imprint of Macmillan Publishing Company, from *The Last of the Mohicans* by James Fenimore Cooper, illustrated by N. C. Wyeth. Copyright 1919 Charles Scribner's Sons; copyright renewed 1947 Carolyn B. Wyeth.

40   W. W. DENSLOW: From *The Wizard of Oz*. Photograph: Robert D. Rubic

42   WINSLOW HOMER: *Boys in a Pasture*. Photograph: © 1988 Museum of Fine Arts, Boston

44   JOHN SINGER SARGENT: *The Daughters of Edward D. Boit*. Photograph: © 1988 Museum of Fine Arts, Boston

49   SARGENT: *Mrs. George Swinton*. Photograph: © 1988 The Art Institute of Chicago. All rights reserved.

49   SARGENT: *Mrs. Charles Thursby*. Photograph: © The Newark Museum

52   SARGENT: *Madame X*. Photograph: © 1979 by The Metropolitan Museum of Art

53   SARGENT: *Asher Wertheimer* and *Ena and Betty, Daughters of Mr. and Mrs. Wertheimer*. Photographs: John Webb

56   SARGENT: *Carnation, Lily, Lily, Rose*. Photograph: John Webb

77   AMEDEO MODIGLIANI: *Head*. Photograph: David Heald

80   PIERRE-AUGUSTE RENOIR: *Maternité*. Photograph: Courtesy of Sotheby's, Inc., New York

84   RENOIR: *Algerian Landscape: The Ravin de la Femme Sauvage*. Photograph: © Réunion des Musées Nationaux

85   RENOIR: *Bather*. Photograph: Routhier

89   RENOIR: *The Swing*. Photograph: © Réunion des Musées Nationaux

98   HILAIRE GERMAIN EDGAR DEGAS: *Drapery*, study for *Semiramis Building Babylon*. Photograph: © Réunion des Musées Nationaux

99   DEGAS: *Scene of War in the Middle Ages*. Photograph: © Réunion des Musées Nationaux

106   DEGAS: *Waiting* (second version). Photograph: © Réunion des Musées Nationaux

107   DEGAS: *Ballet Rehearsal on Stage*. Photograph: © Réunion des Musées Nationaux

109   DEGAS: *Nude Woman Drying Her Foot*. Photograph: © Réunion des Musées Nationaux

Index

Numbers in italics refer to illustrations.

A Note on the Type

The text of this book was set in Sabon, a type face designed by Jan Tschichold (1902–1974), the well-known German typographer. Based loosely on the original designs of Claude Garamond (c. 1480–1561), Sabon is unique in that it was explicitly designed for hot-metal composition on both the Monotype and Linotype machines as well as for film setting. Designed in Frankfurt, Sabon was named for the famous Lyon punchcutter Jacques Sabon, who is thought to have brought some of Garamond's matrices to Frankfurt.

Just Looking was composed by The Sarabande Press, New York, New York, printed and bound by Amilcare Pizzi, S.P.A., Milan, Italy, and designed by Peter A. Andersen.